OPTIONS TRADING CRASH COURSE

THE DEFINITIVE BEGINNER'S GUIDE TO MAKE MONEY WITH TRADING OPTIONS AND BECOME AN EXPERT IN 7 DAYS OR LESS!

Charles Douglas

Copyright © 2020 Charles Douglas

All rights reserved.

This document is geared towards providing exact and reliable information with regard to the topic and issue covered. The publication is sold with the idea that the publisher is not required to render accounting, officially permitted, or otherwise, qualified services. If advice is necessary, legal or professional, a practiced individual in the profession should be ordered.

In no way is it legal to reproduce, duplicate, or transmit any part of this document in either electronic means or in printed format. Recording of this publication is strictly prohibited, and any storage of this document is not allowed unless with written permission from the publisher. All rights reserved.

TABLE OF CONTENT

ABOUT THE BOOK -- 1

INTRODUCTION -- 2

CHAPTER ONE --- 4

    Options Crash Course --- 4

CHAPTER TWO -- 21

    Understand The Options Market From Scratch. ------------------ 21

CHAPTER THREE -- 29

    The Basics Of Options Trading And Investing ------------------ 29

CHAPTER FOUR --- 37

    The Purchase Of Trading Stock Options ------------------------ 37

CHAPTER FIVE --- 46

    Advanced Trading Strategies ---------------------------------- 46

CHAPTER SIX -- 52

    The Advantages of Trading Options Over Stocks ---------------- 52

CHAPTER SEVEN -- 60

    Strategies To Make The Very Best Use Of Your Investment Capital. ------------ 60

CHAPTER EIGHT -- 72

Steps to Choose the Right Stock Options ---------- 72

CHAPTER NINE ---------- 79

How To See Patterns In The Market ---------- 79

CHAPTER TEN ---------- 90

Risk Management ---------- 90

CHAPTER ELEVEN ---------- 101

The Most Common Investor Mistakes ----------101

CONCLUSION ---------- 109

ABOUT THE BOOK

EFFECTIVE GUIDE TO OPTIONS TRADING CRASH COURSE

Find out how this beginner-oriented but thorough guide really works! Trading options: The Ultimate Beginner's Manual: Guidelines to Obey, Mistracks to Stop, Quick but Rentable Methods To Make Money Trading Options: why do you miss it if you don't even invest in options and how the mechanism works. Trading options are not an easy job and entail a major risk. However, you should stick to some guidelines that can help you cut losses drastically, protect your investments, and make your investment journey relatively profitable.

INTRODUCTION

Option trading is another investment vehicle that, when practiced carefully, can give you large returns. To start learning some basic options trading, you must know which options are and how trading options work.

Alternatives are simply contracts between the buyer and the seller at a fixed price and validity period for an asset such as stocks or futures. The trade options are easily drawn to small investors because they can exchange a very large portion with just a small amount of money as capital. Nonetheless, great risks come with it, so do not spend more than you can afford to lose when investing in this company. Experts suggest that it is wise to invest only in options trading with risk capital.

You need extensive knowledge and experience in options trading to start this highly risky type of investment. If you know how to evaluate stocks, you can be a good trader of options. Important and useful information about optional trading principles can be found in different books and on web resources, but it is not possible to learn any information overnight. Seminars on trading options will also help you make good money from this project.

The fundamentals of trading options are options for positioning and call, short and long positions, intrinsic and time-value and hedging, and speculation. Options are riskier than bonds, as their initial value decreases as the day goes by before they are worthless when they mature; the earlier they are sold, the better. Remember that the people who are always nearest to the money trading have the lowest risk, and only their versatility is the ultimate power of options.

Trading options, on the other hand, often provide several advantages over other types of investment. In contrast to stock trading, trading options offer limited risk with unlimited potential for profit. Most investors do use portfolio insurance options. We benefit from flexible contracts to cover their exposure from a stock market crash.

Another thing you should know about the simple options trading is where to contract for share options. While the majority of options are exchanged through public exchanges, it can also be negotiated between two parties in what is known as the countermarket.

To start your business in the field of trading, the most important thing you must note is to pick and be very successful in a certain area of your market. You can also select stock options or an index with a high rate of trading and liquidity. Make sure your standards are reasonable when setting your investment goals. Never underestimate the risks and losses you face.

In addition to the basic knowledge of option trading previously mentioned, an options trader will also know different options strategies. Option pricing can be used to test the risk and reward profiles of different options strategies that will help you understand the business of trading options better. For retail trading, only a simple options strategy is needed.

CHAPTER ONE

OPTIONS CRASH COURSE

Currency exchange trading is a money-oriented sector. It takes place as currencies are traded from all over the world. Inside the forex market, you can buy (long), sell (short) currency, and make money, as long as the price difference favors your position.

You can opt, when entering the foreign exchange market, to enter a long trade for a country's currency and then sell it at a higher price to make a profit from it. For instance, you can buy the Japanese yen, and you can close this order for profit once the yen/dollar ratio increases.

The currency market, as well as the stock market, have some parallels, as both works to generate profit by purchasing and selling, but there are also significant distinctions. Indeed, the currency market has a higher liquidity point. In other words, you have more money changing hands every day.

Another major difference in comparing the currency with the stock market is that there is no international currency exchange in a specific location and is always open to trade from Monday to Friday. The foreign currency market operates between banks and brokers from different countries and offers you 24-hour exposure during the week of trade.

Another distinction between the stock market and the forex is that Forex trade offers you much greater bond leverage than the stock market. When anyone wants to enter the foreign currency market, he or she can expect higher income as long as he or she is trained and knows how and why. On the other hand, you might also lose substantially more money.

For people who are starting out in the foreign currency market, many brokers are offering them the opportunity to trade with mini-Forex accounts. It provides them with a lower minimum deposit, usually $100, on the forex market. It makes it easier for people still to learn how to trade in money, lower the chances of losing a lot of money, and understand how Forex works before committing large sums of money.

You would want to learn some simple words before you agree to exchange a foreign currency. The development of foreign trade skills can sometimes be a challenge for the new trader, but it does not involve rocket science, as a number of well-managed strategies are used to achieve profitability.

Once you start trading the foreign currency market, the first thing you must note is the appearance of symbols, consisting of two parts:

The first section refers to one currency, and the second section refers to the second currency being exchanged. The word "euro," for example, means "pound" and "US dollar." It is critical to understand the meaning of each symbol as you cannot afford to waste time thinking about this when you have split-second decisions ahead.

What Are Options?

What are the opportunities when we think about trading shares? On this day of tight money and the tremendous swings in the stock market, I decided to look at this issue to see if it is worth my while. The first thing I have to do is really understand what they are.

Initially, options are nothing more than contracts for purchasing or selling particular goods. The company is a financial good, which is the underlying value or instrument of the transaction.

Now, like most contracts, it includes very precise information. For you to know what you can find in the contract, we will describe three different terms. Something is known as the strike price. Another term is used, and the expiration date is the third term.

The term strike price refers to the financial product's specific price. The word used does not mean that we have worn the commodity out. Here we mean that the product was used. In the final term, the date of expiration means when the option no longer has any interest or meaning, and the commodity or option simply no longer exists.

There are two kinds of options. The first is known as a call option. The second kind of option is known as a put option. You can choose which choice you want to buy or get rid of. You must agree on what your priorities are as an options trader.

Option Trading Strategies

Although options trading is often seen as risky (and definitely can be), typically, it is both safer and much more profitable than stock trading. The great thing about options trading is that it makes it possible to build a wide variety of strategies with different risk profiles. While courier fees for trading options are substantially higher than for almost any other form of trading, the tremendous profitability available is easily compensated.

The explanation that selling options have been considered to be highly risky is because many traders, motivated by sheer greed, have found maximum returns in the shortest period. Insanely massive profits are certainly possible, but crash and burning are unavoidable unless handled with decided motive. The secret to effective trading of options is to "own" a strategy, understand it thoroughly and use it reliably and with clearly established exchange rules.

Below are (in my opinion) the best trading options to reduce risk and offer very respectable profits:

Selling Credit Spreads - You will increase your portfolio by 10-15% each month with almost no work and about 30 minutes a week. Performance depends on consistency and is not a technique suitable for hyperactive traders or those who want to over-analyze it all. What you need to learn is how to do basic market trend analysis and a carefully chosen stock list. This technique is incredibly lucrative and simpler than a rodeo bull (and much less painful).

Selling Naked Puts. This strategy only really works on an upward trend market and has a slightly higher margin requirement than credit distribution. Similar returns can be obtained, and the risk profile is just as low. The best thing is that you get your income upfront, much like credit spreads.

Buying and selling DITM (Deep-in-the-money) options. This is a great swing trading strategy that allows you to buy stocks effectively for about half the cost and double your profit. Since your companies are all short-term (3-10 days), you are not concerned with dividends or other considerations related to buying and holding stock, but you make profit, since the price movement of the option you purchased is precisely balanced by the stock price movement.

Selling Covered Calls. If you own an inventory, you can effectively reduce the inventory cost by selling covered calls every month on that inventory. This is a method without which stock traders should not do so, but do not use it if you own stock for sentimental purposes-stock trading must be your business. If you get called out sometimes and eventually sell your stock, you can move on to the next quickly.

Complex strategies, like straddles, strangles, iron condors, and butterflies. These are all low risk, highly profitable strategies. Their only disadvantages are that they are all expensive (either expensive options or higher broker fees because of the number of trades involved).

Rules to Follow For Successful Options Trading

Nobody happily goes into selling options. The reality is that it needs loads of preparation and expertise and a deep dedication to market forecasts and benefits. You are not going to get there overnight, either you have the right to trade options frequently without losing sight of benefit targets, or you are actively educating yourself with content to improve your options trades. For our beginners, here is an overview of the options and why you should strengthen your portfolio by providing trade choices:

Options are a demand reserve. You can reserve the right to purchase or reserve the right to sell this asset, which is called a call option. The call options are a long strategy, meaning that they benefit from the price rises when the stock is raised because you are now entitled to buy at a lower reserved price. The bigger part is that you can make the same benefit when you purchase a call option, as someone who purchased the stock, with just a fraction of the initial investment.

Therefore an extra flexibility is one of the benefits of options. You simply can buy the option and do the same thing instead of being obliged to work with shares that force you to throw out thousands of dollars to earn money from a stock rally. They are a key tool for price forecasting.

Trading options also offer greater versatility than stock trading. There are only three strategies when trading stocks: purchase, sell, and keep. For options, the arsenal is massive and can offer several different strategies to make money if the market rises, falls or goes sideways. There are approaches for each market and option trader from the most liberals, such as the covered call and the calendar, to more nuanced techniques such as back ratios, butterflies, and iron condors.

Once you begin trading, there are three basic rules to note that help keeps you out of trouble:

1. **Don't sell more than you could afford to lose.** This is referred to as risk capital. If you risk more than 2-5% of your account in a single business or risk more than you can in a single paycheck at your workday, you are fast to fail by not shielding yourself from a sufficient risk. Isolate yourself from wealth and stay out of trouble.

2. **Avoid infinite danger positions.** When you are selling a call, defend yourself against future losses by buying another call or the stock itself, rather than risk constant losses.

3. **Educate yourself constantly!** Nobody gets a millionaire with one or two hidden programs or a box set of DVDs and a few extra hours a week. It takes hard work and perseverance, so be prepared to keep a student's mind while going into the field of choice, and you can someday enjoy freedom and prosperity without having to maintain 9 to 5 retailers as many.

Types of options

The cost of purchasing options is restricted to the premium paid. On the other hand, the income potential is infinite, making trading possibilities attractive.

An option is a contract that gives the investor the right to purchase or sell assets (raw materials, precious metals, securities, currencies, indices, etc.) at a given price and maturity without being bound by an obligation. On the other hand, if the buyer so demands and receives a premium, the seller is obliged to satisfy his obligations under the contract.

There are two classic types of options, called plain vanilla options:

Call option- Gives the right to purchase an asset at a strike price and maturity (maturity, expiration date) at a certain amount; the price to be paid is called an insurance premium. The option holder depends on a rise in the potential asset price.

Put option- Gives the right to a certain price and maturity to sell a house. The buyer, therefore, expects the asset price to decrease.

- The option contract contains the following elements:
- type - the right to buy (call) or sell (put) an asset
- determines the size of the asset (for example 1000 shares)
- the price at which the option would be exercised
- maturity/period of execution
- premium - the price of the option

From a maturity point of view, options are divided into European forms, in which only maturity is possible. The right can be exercised in the American type of option at any time before the end date. And the form of Bermuda is less common – it can be exercised on many pre-determined dates.

The options are categorized into at-the-money options, where they correspond with two prices, depending upon the actual value of the strike price and the actual asset price. In the money options, the strike price is lower than the present one for CALL options, and in the case of PUT-higher. Outsourcing options – their stunning price for CALL options is higher and vice versa, lower for PUT than the current asset price.

In addition to the classic options, the so-called exotic options, such as:

One-touch option– the buyer will receive the value of the option if the pre-determined price is reached before the option expires.

Double No-Touch Option — for this option, there are two price thresholds-below and above the existing one, so if the premium is not transferred, the consumer earns his reimbursement.

Dual one-touch option – a variation of the above, the buyer gets the value of the option when the price reaches one of the barriers.

Knock-in option-when the price reaches a point; the option starts operating as a standard vanilla option.

Knock-Out- an easy choice for vanilla, which stops if prices hit a certain point.

The cost of buying options is restricted to the premium charged. On the other hand, the income potential is infinite, making trading possibilities attractive. Things are exactly the opposite when selling options, and therefore, it is not recommended to be practiced by inexperienced investors.

Options Trading in Extremely Volatile Markets

The latest bond crisis (2008) rocked not just the financial system and the global economy, but also countless traders of options worldwide. Options traders who used to profit from their banks in the years before this market crisis did not seem to function in this market anymore, as none of their options strategies worked. So what about extremely volatile markets, and how should one profit under such conditions by trading options?

Extremely unpredictable market conditions not only create unpredictable short-term stock price swings but also open up the retail pressure on individual stock options because of lower cash and market-makers' profits. This combined impact made it not only doubly difficult for options traders to benefit. Volatile options strategies, which were intended to satisfy these requirements as a result of their ability to profit from the strong rise or fall of the market and their potential to benefit from increased volatility, have struggled to deliver consistently high profits due to higher premium costs and the broad bid extension, absorbing most profits. Unanticipated rallies often generate crunch volatility in the measure of losses by decaying the premium for long legs at express level. Short-term (weekly, monthly) aggressive strategies went worse because not only were short-term price fluctuations almost difficult to forecast, but the high premium and bid spreads, if not any, of the profits even if the stock went in the anticipated direction.

So what works in an extremely volatile market condition such as this one?

First of all, let's look at all the different ways to trade options. There are 3 main options trading methodologies; Swing Trading, Position Trading, and Day Trading.

Swing trading is a directional trading strategy, which attempts to pick stocks that shift rapidly and strongly into a predictable direction in a short period of time and then execute bullish or bearish options strategies to make use of these movements. As mentioned before, it is like swimming against the tide to try and benefit from directional swing trading in an extremely volatile market. Not only are directions hard to predict, but the high premium options and the gaping bid task all work against it.

Positions trading is more difficult than Swing trading as it primarily seeks to benefit from the uncertainty or premium decay by constructing a variety of options and/or stocks (although there are also tactical trading strategies) to achieve hedged market neutrality. In this market downturn, position trading has yielded some very lucrative returns for me as volatility grew, and premiums for options were strong. This puts in favor of options traders the inconveniences of an extremely volatile market situation. Dynamically hedged delta-neutral, as well as delta-gamma-neutral positions, are part of this. Both of these tactics aim at neutralizing market volatility to ensure that sudden movements do not dramatically impact your position, while the place safe enters your pockets with the high premium options on the short legs.

Day Trading is an extremely competitive form of trading options in which options are acquired and sold within one day quite rapidly to benefit from a minor intraday price increase or volatility increase. This strategy was very difficult to take advantage of under market conditions because rates do not adjust sufficiently within a day to make significant profits. But day trading in the hands of seasoned veterans in highly unpredictable situations such as this market crisis is extremely lucrative as the Dow itself has created intraday trading spreads of up to 10 percent! Indeed, this is the sort of exchange and price range that is not possible in normal market conditions. Day Trading also takes the form of simply buying, shortening, or making a call and covering it quickly when it is profitable. Day trading often avoids extreme uncertainty that too often scare swing traders in this market turmoil. Sudden, good news also diverges the Dow dramatically and lifts it more than 10 percent higher. This will reduce all your gains if you've been investing overnight in the opposite direction. However, day trading is extremely risky for beginners in trading options because the price movements are so rapid and dynamic that when things happen, beginners may not know what to do and can do it quickly. This is therefore not recommended for beginners.

Myths About Options Trading

Options are one of the most lucrative financial instruments. Trading options can look very complicated for a beginner, and a great deal of experience is required to really reward them. Yet once you understand it, you will make a lot of money. There are many types of options, with Exchange trading options being the main one. Those are options like stock options, asset options, index options, or future contract options. Many traders prefer stock options because the rewards are high. If they correctly forecast, they will make profit, whether the stock price rises or falls.

To understand how options work, look at the example below: You decided you would like to buy some gold. You go to a gold dealer and see the demand for an ounce of $450. Since this is the last week of the month, you still wait for your payment, so you can't yet buy it. You agree with the dealer to give you the opportunity to buy it at the same price by next week. He needs a fee to do so, so you deposited $50. You are now the option holder and have the right to buy the necklace, but you are not obligated to buy it in the agreed time.

Within the next couple of days, the country's economy will collapse, the markets will collapse, and investors will buy gold, bringing their prices up to $900 an ounce. You just run into the gold dealer, who is obliged to sell you gold at the agreed price. You just earned $400 if you choose to sell the gold at its present market value. Nonetheless, if there were no recession and the gold price fell to say $300, you wouldn't have to buy it at $450 and lose just $50.

Trading options is extremely profitable, and many complicated contracts are concluded. You must make sure you know the fundamentals of the trade before you consider investing in the options. You should also ensure that you have capital specifically reserved for trading options. In the beginning, trade only in small amounts until you have ample experience to put more per trade.

Myth #1: Options trading is risky.

Truth: It may be for those who have not been prepared. For those who understand these instruments, options are a way of reducing trade risk. Options provide a very lucrative income source for those who practice their tactics. Know before you earn.

Myth #2: Options are difficult to understand.

Truth: The more you commit to learning, the greater the understanding, like anything. You don't have to learn anything, just enough to make them work for you. Actually, it's not that hard if you have a strong mentor.

Myth #3: Traders must be familiar with many stocks and strategies.

Truth: Not so. Not so. Master just one or two great strategies with a big stock. Know the complexities and actions, and several times a day, you will make an outstanding living. Keeping it simple is important for gradual wealth accumulation with choices.

Myth #4: Options trading is only for professional, experienced traders.

Truth: Trading options is now commonplace for the masses, especially in recent years. Traders see the benefits of lower risk, lower investment, and higher option leverage. Computerized trading platforms offer both ready access.

Myth #5: Options trade execution is a rip-off.

Truth: The assumption is that market makers have rigged the system, through which they only invested and improved retail traders. In fact, technology has eliminated this outdated order flow system by transparently contesting various exchanges for the same order.

Myth #6: Options create market crashes.

Truth: The prices are driven by greedy bankers and operators. In fact, options can hedge against these bubbles. The famous Dutch tulip bubble of 1637 was the very first one to hit about $2,500 in the U.S. before the market became sober.

Myth #7: Trading options is a function of greed.

Truth: Quite the opposite. After the recent downturn of the market, more investors play an active role in their financial future rather than allowing their mentor to lose their money. The astute trader uses capital defense, profit increase, and control options.

Myth #8: This is not a good time to invest in the market.

Truth: Traders can make money from either bull or bear markets by using options. Unlike stock aimed at profiting from equity growth, effective traders are just as happy to buy and sell, sell, and purchase as trends evolve.

Myth #9: Trading options is akin to gambling.

Truth: Maybe for the uneducated. The investor/trader aims to benefit from market growth or the overall prosperity of the economy. Gambling is a zero-sum game; on the other hand, literally redistributing capital from loser to winner. Another myth has vanished.

Myth #10: You must spend thousands on trading courses to be successful.

Truth: You might invest that quickly, but these courses appear to offer you more courses most often. Find a mentor who cares about your career, assesses your needs properly, and coaches you throughout. These teachers respect their gold weight.

When it comes to trading on the stock markets, almost everyone has a different opinion and will give you different advice. And while some of these tips can be very useful, they are definitely suitable for one type of investor and not particularly suitable for others.

Options trading is very specific. It requires two main things. First, you are right that a certain asset will move strongly in one direction (of course, you know this direction), and second, the expected strong movement will occur within the time limit set by the options.

In fact, let's start a little further. What are options?

These are derivatives that give you the right (but not the obligation) to buy or sell a certain asset at a pre-determined price until a certain date. Of course, you pay for this right, through the premium included in the option price, which is the difference between the current price of the asset and the price at which you can exercise your right.

There are four important elements to options - type, maturity, premium, and the exercise price.

The options are divided into two types - call and put options. With the purchase of the former, you bet on an increase in the price of the asset on which they are based, and with the latter - for a decrease. Usually, one option is based on the purchase or sale of 100 shares of the company.

The second element of the option is a premium. This is the price that the investor pays for the right to buy the asset at a certain price in the future. The price is paid for the convenience of investors being able to lose only as much as the option costs. The premium is defined as the difference between the exercise price of an option and the current price at which the asset is traded.

Usually, the longer the options, the higher the trading premium set in them.

The exercise price is the set price at which investors will be able to exercise their option on the maturity date. Depending on the exercise price, options are divided into "cash options" and "non-cash options." cash options are those options whose exercise price is lower than the current price of the asset when it comes to call options, and the exercise price is higher than the current asset price in put options.

The third element of the option is maturity. This is the date the option expires. On this date, it must either be practiced or deleted. In case the investors do not exercise their option, the difference between the current price and the exercise price is usually transferred to their account at the last moment of the options expiration if the difference is positive for call options and negative for put options.

One of the biggest advantages of the options, as already mentioned, is that they bring losses to investors only up to the amount invested. Unlike margin trading, in which investors can lose funds many times their own (that is, owe money to their brokers), options do not have such a danger.

We will now look at some common myths about options trading:

Myth 11: Options trading is riskier than stock trading

This is one of the statements that does not contain the whole truth. People think that the options are riskier because with them, a loss of 100% is an opportunity. In practice, however, options can be used to hedge investors' positions, or in other words, to prevent excessive losses.

Here is an example. Let's say you have 100 shares of Tesla, and the company is facing results that you think will be good. These 100 shares cost you about $ 27,000, based on the company's stock price of $ 270. This means that if the company's shares fall by 10%, with possibly worse results, it would cost you $ 2,700.

It is possible to buy a call option with a strike of $ 270, for the amount of $ 1,350. This means that if the company's shares fall 10% before they expire, the largest amount you can lose is $ 1,350.

That is, you can buy two options, or have exposure to 200 shares of Tesla, for a maximum loss of $ 2,700, as much as you would lose from 100 shares, with a possible decline of 10%.

However, if the company's shares rise, your profits will be higher.

Myth1 2: You need to have a lot of knowledge and apply complex strategies to trade options.

Yes, there are also options traders who follow very complex strategies. However, this does not mean that you cannot use options for very traditional things, such as speculating or limiting your losses without having any financial knowledge.

For example, you can buy call options if you think an asset will rise in price, as well as put options if you expect them to fall in price. If a key event involving an asset is imminent, it is very easy to apply simple strategies to benefit from a potentially more serious move in either direction.

Myth 13: It takes a lot of money to trade options

This can't be further from the truth. An option contract is based on 100 shares of your chosen company. The price of the option can be in the range of 100 or 200 dollars, no matter how expensive the asset. Of course, with such cheap options, there will probably be a serious premium in the price.

Myth 14: Time always works against you with options

This is true if you buy options. However, if you sell options, things are quite the opposite. Time is on your side, and the closer you get to the maturity of the options, the more of the premium will go into your pocket.

Myth 15: You need a special account to trade options

Yes, it is true that in order to trade options, you must fill out a special declaration, and your account must be approved for this. But for accounts with some brokers, options trading is a standard feature, as long as it is allowed by the financial institution.

CHAPTER TWO

UNDERSTAND THE OPTIONS MARKET FROM SCRATCH.

Options trading seems often clouded in darkness when it is simply a simple method for investment, employed by major investment firms and individuals. Sometimes the world media enjoys spreading fear because a stranger has used derivatives such as options for secret and stupid investments and has thereby lost a great deal of money. This form of press reporting has led to a poor reputation for options trading. The reality is that most prudent traders use options to reduce risks rather than raise them.

Why is this going to work? An investment firm may have bought a large number of shares for its clients in a specific company. When the market collapses for any reason, the price of the company's stock will be impacted, even though the company is fundamentally sound. Most investors seek to sell the shares as soon as possible but sometimes can not find a buyer to avoid the carnage. However, if the investor company acquires a 'put' contract on its shares, this provides a solid guarantee that they will be able to sell the shares at a fixed price, even if they are trading at that time much lower. The company typically purchases a form of short-term insurance to ensure that its investment is covered to a certain extent. It thus protects its customers against heavy losses and protects its reputation at the same time.

On the other hand, a big corporation like Sony plans in the near future to develop a new gadget. Expectations will generate a lot of interest in the stock, and thus, the share prices increase. For this scenario, an investment company might want to buy large stock blocks for its customers but at the best price possible. Therefore, before the hysteria starts, the client can obtain the right to buy the stock at a fixed price in the future (this is called a 'Call Option' agreement). This is then a guaranteed price that can be passed on to its customers. Of course, if the inventory has increased prices during that period, customers will benefit from the investment firm's foresight and make an immediate profit. If the price is high, on the other hand, the company actually permits the right to expire and buy the stock at a lower price. In any case, it ends up with the best possible consumer exchange, and its credibility is, of course, secured.

Individual investors may use the same strategies as large investment companies, but obviously in much lesser amounts. It doesn't vary in any respects from taking a mortgage for the purchase of a home. You use a small amount of your own money in conjunction with money from the bank (which you do not actually receive or touch) to control a property, which is much more expensive than you can afford. If the housing market is rising, you profit entirely from the growth, even if your own financial contribution is relatively low. This is the leverage theory. You can use options to monitor the ownership of large stock blocks that you don't really have to buy, and also protect your stocks against major swings in the market.

Flexibility is the true beauty of options trading. In the case of market volatility, you might sell options, and thus become a kind of insurance salesman, rather than buy 'insurance' for your stock. You can even do this by combining various options contracts to make sure you are also protected. These strategies (with crazy titles, including 'credit spreads' and 'iron condors' and 'butterfly spreads') simply adjust a theme to gain value while mitigating risk.

Understanding the Stock Options Trading System

Trading in stocks can be a successful career. However, there is also a chance-if your profile can be gold in one minute, and it can become stone in the next. Anyone engaging in trading stock options knows how risky it is. The risk is a permanent trading aspect, and entering the market means that all the risks involved are known and taken into account.

Today, technology has progressed so much that traders worldwide have the latest tools to make educated decisions. Another such tool is the app for stock options. Trading of stock options consists of revolutionary software that increases the art of trading to a completely new level.

This specific software permits individuals involved in the stock market to make essential decisions in real-time. Certain individuals debate whether personal experience and intuition are really necessary in the difficult world of stock trading, but it is also a requirement of traders to combine in their teams the latest technology that can put them a step in front of their competitors. It takes some time before a trader can be confident in doing business according to his computations.

The programming of the stock option has the capacity to do several calculations in just one minute. Software like options applications is certainly valuable in a trade that requires real-time growth. It is also important to find the best trading options software to perform this job.

There are many program forms, and some of them are even free. There are several ways for traders to exchange software goods. Such software tools work in different ways and give traders various advantages. The book addresses various software programs involved in trading options.

Stock exchange has been divided into different sales. Another of these sales is the sale of stock options. A stock option is to buy and sell stocks for some time at a fixed price. The key option form is the call option. Your privilege expires at a certain point in time, but it allows you to buy the stock at $40 per share even if the price is adjusted within the time frame for your "right" profit. This right is referred to as the call option.

Another type of option is known as the put option. A put option allows you to sell the stock for a fixed price for a specified period of time. Businesses generally provide their employees with stock options as a kind of compensation. Employees are entitled to buy shares at a fixed price per share at a later date. In summary, workers have calling options.

Trading stock options is much more difficult than straight trading stocks. When we trade an option, you have to offer a strike price, an expiry month, and the type of trading options needed (CALL or PUT), and your first position will be on the side. For traders, stock options can be extremely risky.

Options are developed in two ways: you can make money, or you can lose money. When the stock price falls, a call option is worth nothing, but it can be very worthwhile if the prices start to increase. If the share price increases, a put option will not be worth anything, and it will be worth it if the price declines. In order to buy stock options, it is necessary to balance the odds.

Basics of Stock Options Trading

Before joining any kind of stock contract, it is absolutely necessary for everyone to have at least some basic information and knowledge. There are several topics to understand, and here the issue of "Stock Options Trading" is explained.

If spoken in the simplest way, the stock option is some kind of agreement between all sides, i.e., the buyer and the seller, where they have the right to purchase and sell shares and stocks at a certain price. Just as all stock options have an expiry date, and the purchasing or sales process must be completed before that date. Yet this contract simply doesn't compel you to buy or sell any stock outright. It can now be understood that stock options are an entirely different kind of security where you can invest and deal with your assets. In capital markets/exchanges, stock options are also exchanged and handled. The Chicago Board Options Exchange (CBOE) is the largest stock exchange dealing with stock options trading in the United States.

This topic can be a difficult challenge for entrants to the stock exchange as it involves several words and definitions that are typically fresh in nature. As stated before, this right or offer lays no foundation for the purchase or selling of your stock. For instance, if you're currently in this deal, you will be able to buy shares two months from now at the predefined price. The turning point here is that the value of the stock you bought increases, it will be your benefit and the rates will fall, and it's your loss entirely because you will lose the entire premium. To get the maximum benefit out of stock options trading, you must be fully conversant with the following tips.

Do research – The first and fundamental way to learn this subject is to do some study. Be aware of the lingo used in this topic. Know the meanings of various terms like calls, puts, long call, short call, long put, short put, long synthetic, short synthetic, call back spread, put back spread, call bull spread, put bull spread, covered call, protective put, collar, call bear spread, put bear spread, long straddle, short straddle, short strangle, long strangle, long guts, short guts, call time spread, put time spread, call ration vertical, put ration vertical, long call butterfly, short call butterfly, long put butterfly, short put butterfly, long condor and short condor, etc.

Sharpness- Use the internet as the biggest source of your Stock Options Trading knowledge. You can obtain a lot of information by reading newsletters, forum posts, and material on websites. This helps you understand the underlying technicalities of the topic of stock options trading.

Tutorials: One of the best ways established so far to get in the stock market is to take some lessons or tutorials successfully. Here too, the Internet can be our simple instructor by letting you know the fundamentals of investing in stocks, and then, there are videos, illustrations, animated advertisements that are helpful to anyone who wishes to get into stock options and get big returns.

Things To Know Before You Trade

Option trading provides various advantages from trading other securities such as commodities, forexes, shares, etc. To fully understand the power and versatility that options offer, one needs to have a strong understanding of certain key dynamics that help sustain trading capital and eventually structure risk in a positive way to reduce losses and optimize profitable positions.

One of the most common concerns for new traders who jumped too quickly into options market seems to be, "I don't understand why I lost money even though the direction of trading was in my favor." I was also puzzled by this behavior when I initially began trading and learned why, so that I could 'pull' these negative aspects of the option agreement and turn it into profit.

A quick breakdown and short explanation of some of the more important aspects of options trading might help to clarify:

Risk Management. It is possibly one of the most misunderstood trading elements in general, but particularly for trading options. Too often, newer dealers start with a small account (say 2000 dollars) and place trades at risk of more than 300 dollars of their capital. Let's look at the scenario to understand why he is a murderer: if I were to suggest that I risk a potential $3 return for every $1 dollar (good system in its own right). Well, if I risk $300 for every business I make, it will take just about six bad trades to wipe my full account off! Let's look at a particular scenario: I could handle my risk much more efficiently if I assigned a fixed percentage of my entire capital base (remember that the capital base is always changing). For instance, if I risk a percentage of my capital on my $2000 account, say, 3 percent, I might risk $60 per trade, and my risk amount rises as my account grows larger and vice versa. One would argue that this is a much more stable method that allows you to stand up against a greater number of losing businesses when you win.

Broker Commissions. For smaller traders, broker commissions could be another silent killer. Please bear in mind that discussions with your broker for better brokerage rates will be an ongoing discussion. If your broker is doing a good amount, yet you still have the same fee structure as when you started trading with them, call them on the telephone and see what they can do for you – you may be amazed at the outcome.

The Romans. No, not the great philosophers; we speak of the Greeks alternative, the key ones: Delta, Gamma, Theta, Vega. Each of these "Greeks" has an option contract intent. In my video course, we call them 'variables' in the contract...moving time decay pieces, motion percentage, implied volatility, etc. I know it sounds complicated. These words can frighten you a little when you have new options, but I can assure you that once you learn about their purpose, you can use them to structure your risk, which is mainly what trading is about.

Hedging. Hedging structures your risk essentially in your portfolio, in which you protect your positional bias by taking a share of the "other" side of the trade, if it is against you. For instance, I was thinking that stock "XYZ" would break up, and I purchased 6 call options. If I was wrong, I would want to cover myself in trade and, at the same time, buy 3 Put options when "XYZ" crashes occur, and I lose my money on the call options I bought. If "XYZ" collapses (that means the stock goes down very fast), at least I have my 3 Put options to make money - Balance my losses (and even benefit sometimes) as my call options expire without interest. The example above is quite simple, but it gives you a sense of how Hedging can protect your capital in the event of unexpected movements in the market.

Implied Volatility. Implied uncertainty is a central player in the pricing environment. With reference to the aforementioned argument by newer dealers, "I do not understand why I lost money, although the direction of the trade was in my favor" ... well, implicit uncertainty in this situation is more often than not the culprit. Before the market to put a price tag on an option contract, the amount of potential risk associated with the holding of the contract must be calculated-this is the role of implied volatility, in short. Simply stated, if implied volatility increases, the price of the option increases, and vice versa. What if you purchase an option that already has incredibly great implied volatility, then the inventory moves higher while the implied volatility actually decreases? Yeah, that's one of the reasons why younger traders don't get the most out of the options market. The trick is to place implicit uncertainty on your side, so you automatically know when to purchase an option and what the price is.

CHAPTER THREE

THE BASICS OF OPTIONS TRADING AND INVESTING

Ordinary people believe that the trading of options is often risky. It is reputed to be risky, but this is a misconception about options trading. While trading options can be highly risky, it can be highly profitable if you are equipped with good trading skills and strategies. It involves risk and insecurity, just like any other type of offline or online trading. Risks and risks are higher when you have no idea what you are doing.

I would like to start with the basics of trading options, its implementation in the USA, and how it is lucrative for many people and loses out to others. Later in this book, I'm thinking about some of the main things you need to know about trading options, which might help you win a day on the market.

An option is an arrangement in which one gives someone else the right to buy or sell something in the future. If you buy a Dow call option, the Dow index futures options mean you buy the right/privilege to purchase this underlying Dow future at a certain price at a certain point in the future. This definite price is referred to as the "strike price," while the actual time is called the "expiry date."

This trade can also be understood as if an investor buys a put; they essentially sell the market because a call essentially buys the market. Similarly, when an investor sells a put, they mainly buy the market because a call essentially sells the market.

When the market does not allow the price of the options to fall, otherwise, that option is deemed worthless at the expiration date. In order to buy an option in this future, investors pay a so-called "premium." Moreover, if the market will not hit the option's strike price on the expiry date, the buyer will be given the underlying future at that same strike price.

How Options Trading Began

This business company started in the 19th century. The launch of options trading coincided with the launch of stock trading. The situation, however, is different since newspaper ads must be used to identify sales choices. It can be concluded that trading options had not gained ground in the market at that period.

Options trading started officially in 1848, when the Chicago Trade Board was formed, and contracts started in the US. Many exchange options began when trading contracts involving options were launched by Chicago Exchange Board, Kansas City Board of Trade, Minneapolis Grain Exchange, and New York Cotton Exchange.

However, the trading of options was not as common as an alternative for investment in the market. This low popularity is obviously due to the scarcity of the low alternative during that period.

Important developments only happened in the mid-20th century when the Chicago Exchange Board opened and paved the way for the trading of options. The liquidity of options has since expanded enormously, making it a pull to trade options for viewers.

Another significant landmark was reached in 1977, when the Chicago Trading Board began to trade options. In 1985, the NYSE and NASDAQ entered into contracts for stock options.

Until then, selling options has become a common form of investing in the market. This success is attributed to its high liquidity and high leverage. There are a wide variety of products in the market today. Investors may consider options on equities, futures, indexes and currencies. However, options trading is still considered to be one of the most risky kinds of market investing in which you can lose all invested money.

Things you need to know about options trading

As mentioned earlier, options trading is extremely risky if you do not have great skills and fundamental knowledge. It pays a lot to learn more about trading options before you start. If you don't have enough experience and ability, in the first few hours or days of the contract, you may lose the luxury of the king. What you need to find is the right details to make this investment a success. If you get the wrong stuff, you can lose it all. So what are you supposed to do before you start trading? Second, be mindful of the options market.

Investment Tips for Beginners

Are you now joining new portfolios, stocks, and trading ventures? If so, read more carefully to see how you can consider such an important and timely trading options strategy to help you with these new business enterprises. It does not necessarily mean a 100 % guarantee or protection of your assets or your hard-earned money, but it may be a strong beginning for your risk management steps and fads. Many experts would say that options trading can seem the most dangerous of all, but people still want to get into it, given the risks and other possibilities of non-assurance. Why? Why? There is one possible explanation for this: Options contracts and stock options give you leverage variations-a more general term for any strategy used to combine financial gains and losses. And many entrepreneurs and investors alike expect profits to be produced and multiplied.

If you are a novice, you know what to do to learn and appreciate all the risks so that you can deal with them. Of course, you want to make sure that you know exactly where to go before you spend huge sums of money and potentially risk everything. You have to make sure that you understand exactly what the risks are when it comes to something so unpredictable and risky as trading?

Basically, options trading requires a reliable trading strategy for options to make it work for you and your money. Nevertheless, this activity is not intended for those with a poor personality, low trust, low self-reliance, and self-esteem. Otherwise, all your dreams and hopes will be thrown into waste. You should have high levels of confidence in this investment strategy yourself, rather than anyone else. You need to work closely on this because it needs commitment, active involvement, and collaboration, because long as money is at stake and at stake.

Yet don't feel bad because there's also a smart way to make the trading strategies work for you. This is if you prepare, schedule, and bring it all in order. Otherwise, you would probably lose everything with a finger shake, an eye twitch. I'm so sure you don't want to do that, right? If so, you must ensure that you track very closely so that your chosen options trading strategy can be checked and updated and that the market plans are made available to you for any adjustments.

Note that selling options can not necessarily mean investment. Rather, it is like assuming and taking on some business risks-believing you can take advantage of the fluctuations in the market with different conditions. For you to be a good investor, you need to be able to forecast the outcome, evaluate the situation, and determine where the market will take you.

Understanding the Risks of Option Trading

While you are here, you're going to seek out new ideas, such as broadening your horizons with investment vehicles. Truly, one perfect options trading strategy can be found from your own personal experiences during your new journey. When you begin your research efforts for this new mission, this post will at least give you useful and realistic trade options and investment tips to help you get started.

Specify an investment strategy. This action plan must be rational, transparent, and realistic. To make this happen, you have to make it realistic. Setting such a plan in a time frame and restricting its parameters will make it simpler and more available. Start with small steps as you work out greater profits by means of such a trading options strategy.

Investment and trade must be chosen, be it short term or long term, with the main objective in mind: stability, income, or development. You may need to set your priority among these three elements and objectives-whether you are first after protection, income, or development. You have to assume in planning your strategy that this company has its own costs and advantages and that all you will do includes risks and profits.

Consult a professional, an expert, a broker, and an accomplished investor. Whether you meet them in person or on the web, this expert trader will lead you to an investor and trader group. Meeting and contact with these partners can be a perfect way to leverage various tools that can be useful for your requirements for such a robust options trading strategy. Addressing your immediate problems, helping you with our dilemmas, clearing stuff up, providing suggestions and guidance, and providing you some helpful tips are just some of the stuff you can do to take you on the road.

Enter certain options traders clubs and groups throughout all nations. These highly qualified people can easily explain some profitable trading strategies, including important market opportunities and daily trading lessons. Remember to never stop learning, and to encourage yourself to participate regularly in several online live forums can be extremely helpful. After all, both the newbies and the seasoned traders will certainly benefit from this learning experience in the active trade forum-to improve mutual understanding and to share the goodness of this trading strategy venture option. Equip yourself by always keeping you up to date and on the loop. This is also a must know the basic elements of investment and exchange, and you have to learn how to play the game. Yes, there were so many other ways to kick this venture and to keep your investment vehicle going so far. With all these humble efforts, you surely can make everything work for you and your money.

The Basic Difference Between Futures and Options Trading

Futures and options trading may, in reality, be a risky business and only with risk capital that would not alter your lifestyle if your investment is lost. The income potential is nearly infinite, and the loss potential is nearly unlimited. This means that if you're losing a bare future deal, you will lose more cash than you have in the bank. Because of the high leverage, you are responsible for the entire contract sum. There are several ways to reduce your risk, and one of these is to take options away from your role as a hedge against a negative price change, whether it is on the long side or short. Consider some of the variations between future investing and trading in options.

Although I said there are almost infinite downside potentials, this is only valid for an option if you sell the option without holding a different position. If you sold a gold option in June, 900, and the market went to 800; you were then responsible for the 100 points against your place in the gold contract. Your loss will be less the premium that you paid to sell the gold. Due to the volatile nature of the markets, you must understand how much of a trade you are willing to risk and then open up a different position to minimize your downside risk. That is possible for both future and trading options.

1. Premium vs. margin

Options: If you purchase an option, you don't have to make that difference, because you buy the option at a fixed price, which is often called the premium. This premium can decrease over the life of the option if the underlying price of the commodity goes against or stays flat. If you do not exercise this option before the expiry, you will forfeit the premium you paid, and the seller of the option will gain from the amount payable.

Futures: While the premium for a future option does not waste time, the futures contract does not. You should consider the margin on a futures contract as earnings that make you responsible for the entire value of the future deal. This is very risky if you do not open a compensating place to shield you from negative price movements.

2. Risk

Options: As a buyer of options, you are limited to the value of the premium that you paid for the option, and your risk is also considered limited.

Futures: Despite if you buy a futures contract or sell a futures contract, you are responsible for more than the original margin for the deal—this limitless trade risk of this nature.

3. Expiration Dates

The last notable distinction in the trading of futures and options is their expiry date. When you plan to have an option to control the underlying future contract, you should be mindful that it must be delivered around a month before the future is to be delivered. That is for the actual distribution of the goods and does not refer to the measures that are not physical goods and require the expiry dates to be equal to the delivery dates.

As you can see, there are several fundamental differences in the technical aspects of each contract between the future and trading options. Trading these instruments in terms of trading platforms and specialized risk management techniques is a very different matter. Use this book as a basic preliminary to further study futures trading and see whether future and trading options are right for you.

CHAPTER FOUR

THE PURCHASE OF TRADING STOCK OPTIONS

There is plenty of information on the web about options and online brokerage growth. It is not difficult to know the basics about how to trade stock options. You have to control your emotions and manage your money well to start trading.

When you own a company's stock or shares, you have a part of the company. An option is an arrangement or contract, in which one party agrees to deliver something within a given time and for a certain price to another party. An option is a contract that allows you to buy or sell 100 stock shares on a certain date at a certain price.

There are two kinds of choices called puts and calls. The call option requires you to buy a stock until the option expires and requires you to use the put option, which does not require you to sell a stock at the strike price at any point before the expiration date.

How to trade stock options is common because they can help you get more bangs. You may enter a contract of choices, which can be cheaper but have the same, if not better, outcomes, instead of buying an inventory. Trading stock options are for those who have risk and management positions in comfort.

If people sell options, they build protection that hasn't existed before. It is called an options writing and illustrates one of the main sources of options as no organization trades options for problems. When you make a bid, you will be allowed to sell shares sometime before the expiry date at the strike price. You will be obligated to buy shares at the strike price sometime before expiry when you write a quote.

Here is more about how to trade stock options.

• Choices are less risky than inventory holding, but that is not always the case. If you plan to trade options, make sure you fully understand the risks and drawbacks of every trade.

• Options require more consideration and will easily intensify the movement of stocks for your benefit or for your benefit.

• The selling of stock options requires that you understand the market, have an edge, and carry out a strategy.

• Stock options have an expiry date so that you can exercise your options from a certain date to a certain time. If at this time you don't practice them, you lose them.

Actions options are good investments, and many companies offer staff stock options as an incentive for loyalty and also for the attraction of new staff. The stock options are acquired at the strike price or the reduced grant price. If the companies require some time to exercise stocks, costs are likely to increase, and the holder may thus make a profit.

Trading Stock Options Against the Trend

It hits like a ton of bricks when you first know. This is so easy but so real. The rate is about 80 percent of stocks. "Trend is our mate," we all know. Do you smell a woodpile contrarian? Well, when 80%

of the shares move with the trend, only approximately 20% of the stocks or options move against the trend on a typical day. There must be a way of using these advantages. And there are choices.

An option trader can use this information to make a profit from the market trend. The trader will write (sell) a donation. The writer doesn't own the underlying stock (it doesn't claim the option would have been written in a state of undress). It is often called "naked put." If the stock price rises as expected, the trader who writes (sells) the put will hold the writing premium as long as the price doesn't fall below the strike price. Assuming that 80% of the stocks move with the trend, the probability of shares moving against the trend, and the author could be very small. To carry out this form of trade, however, the trader needs to understand well what the short-term and long-term trends are and whether any potential news (reports on sales, negative news, etc.) could revert the stock. This is one of the most risky tactics as the authors will purchase the underlying stock with the buyer of the option if the money is put in, and the option is called.

A way to make money against the trend is to write a covered call much safer for an option trader. If the underlying inventory belongs to the dealer (thus, the interest is "protected" when called off), the call writer option hopes that some other trader believes the base inventory will rise in value as the derivative option. However, if the owner is really conscious of his inventory and thinks his sometimes docile actions will prevent him from having a certain strike price, the call writer will make money when the option expires because it is not in the money and is called away. For example, if there is a longer-term trend, but the shorter-term trend is in a correction phase, the trader will be able to enter the covered call with an expiry date that falls within a period in which the correction will revert to the long-term. The call writer hopes to tempt a trader who doesn't understand the stock as well as him by the prospect of a significant step up into the market. The call writer holds the premium when the option expires, and if things still look good (not much upside movement), he gets ready to do it again and again. Since there are almost every month's optional expiration dates, the return can be quite impressive in the long run. If a covered call writer has no chance and his stock is called off, he can retain all profits and premiums. The only thing he might lose is the expense of an extensive change in the underlying stock.

Keys To Stock Option Trading

Trading stock options provides the professional trader with a greater ability to trade wealth options than virtually any other form of online trading on today's market. The degree of controlled risk and superior leverage enables an experienced trader to make an enormous profit. But an aspiring trader of options must have a solid basis for learning what constitutes an effective options trading method to achieve long-term success with trading options. There are five key keys that any trader of options needs to understand when designing a winning stock options program.

Next, you need to understand how long the premium of the option you find is affected. There are two aspects that you will take into consideration when making stock option trading decisions. The first thing you need to remember is the intrinsic time left on an option. Since options have a limited time span, depending on the specific option you buy from, from 30 days to several years, you must make sure you buy the appropriate option that contains enough time so that your investment will not be depleted until your position has enough time for profit.

The second skill needed to be profitable in trading options is to take time to trade a particular stock option in your trading system and also knowing the statistics on your trade options methodology or trading options establishment by knowing the average holding time of a trading signal. If your typical holding time is seven days, you don't want to buy an option with three months of premium remaining because you will pay extra for the additional period with the purchasing price of the option. Nor would you purchase an option for less than 30 days until time decline erodes the option's value so fast that, even if the underlying stock movements of the option were positive for you, a decline in time would prevent you from realizing an additional gain in the option itself.

Thirdly, an appreciation of the volatility relationship between the market, the underlying share underlying the stock option, and the effect on the value of the option. When the stock market as an index is passed through cycles of uncertainty or low trading levels, the equity shares begin to follow the general trend and start experiencing periods of low overall volatility, which may, in turn, result in derivatives such as stock options being cheap or low premiums. But if the market price increases, it is possible that individual stocks will follow the trend leading to valuation increases as the market shifts in favor of the trader. The next key to how stocks can be traded effectively is a stock option trading scheme that takes account of these key factors while offering clear entry signals, clear exit signals, a fixed trading structure, and a benefit factor higher than your average loss over a number of trades. The ins and outs of various trade agreements are meaningless if you do not have a trading methodology that directs you every step in the trade operation. A robust trading system takes you by the hand and determines every move and leads you to be a steady market winner and successful trader when you do everything.

Finally, you, and your trade psychology, in particular, are the fifth and final key to successfully trading stock options. Human beings and their mental structure are incredibly complex, and it is extremely important that stock options traders not only have a sound stock options, but also the discipline they can sell. You may offer the same precise winning trading scheme to two men, but the results are very similar. The one who has the capacity to remain as separate from his losing businesses as well as his winning businesses while maintaining the discipline to obey the rules of the system irrespective of trade outcome will, in the end, be the biggest winner.

By using these five keys to build your stock options trading approach, you can prevent errors and crashes by other traders of starting options. When you understand time declines, how uncertainty affects the value of a stock option, which determines a reliable stock options trading approach and your own trading psychology, you have a foundation to grow into a good stock options trader.

Reasons to Buy Stock Options

I have several friends who have been investing for many years in the stock market. Many of them return to their companies by about 30 percent a year, but they all want to do more. However, both of them have full-time jobs and have little desire or spare money to make more than that. This is why I plan to invest in stock options and not just stocks.

Trading Stock Options

Currently, I'm not thinking about stock options for employees but stock options that are a form of derivative. If you don't know this kind of alternative, it's OK, not many people are. When I discuss stock options, I have to be careful now because people have become very wary about derivatives since the 2008 stock market crash. When you understand them, though, and note that not much can be evil, the fear begins to go away. Let us, therefore, speak about five reasons why you should consider investing in stock options and not just stocks:

Leverage From Options — Options allow you to manage 100 stock shares per option, without actually purchasing stock. That is why the price change of a stock option is higher and lower when you compare the price change of an underlying stock. In reality, many professionals assume that the option would shift 25 percent for every single percent stock price movement. Naturally, the number varies according to many factors, and many professionals have developed many more sophisticated ways to monitor this ratio.

Minimize Your Portfolio Risk -- If your portfolio only invests in stocks and stock market crashes or decreases. However, you can actually offset or grow your portfolio in a market downswing if you invest wisely in input options. What may you ask? Because a placement option typically increases when its underlying inventory decreases in value and vice versa when the stock increases.

Spend Less -- Options are great because you can buy the right to control a stock for much less than you would pay to actually purchase the stock. For example, you may pay $1,500 at $15 per share to purchase 100 shares of XYZ Corporation, while you may only pay about $300 at $3 per share to purchase stock options of the shares of the same stock. Options are fantastic, as you can buy the option to purchase a stock for less than you cost to buy the stock. For instance, for 100 shares of the XYZ Company, you can pay $1,500 at $15 per share, while for stock options, you are only able to pay around $300 at $3 per share.

Lose Less -- If you buy call options and the stock rises, there is an infinite profit opportunity that also allows you to purchase the stock at the strike price. Even if the stock falls, you just forfeit the option's selling price of $300 instead of a potential loss of $1500. This exact scenario applies, of course, only to call options.

Options Are More Captivating -- Because of the expiration date, many investors find stock options more attractive than stocks. Every alternative has expiry dates and hence has its value, its time value, which gradually erodes. This creates more motivation to look at the alternative and make sure you know what is going on.

How Stock Options Work to Make Big Profits

The stock option is a kind of benefit given to an employee by the company in which he or she has the right, within a given time period, to sell or buy a certain stock in the company in which he or she works for or at a discount price set by his or her employer. Most public and private enterprises demonstrate how stock options work. There are stock options both in public and private businesses due to a host of factors, such as the fact that they are a good way to retain existing employees and attract new ones. They also develop a sense of ownership between the company's employees. Stock options are also a good way for enterprises to keep as much liquidity as possible while providing generous salaries for their employees.

To better understand how stock options work, one must understand that there are two kinds of stock options: the option "put" and the option "call." The 'placement' option grants the buyer the right to sell a portion of an inventory on or before the specified day, while the 'download' option grants the buyer the right to purchase a portion of the inventory at or before the specified date, at a specific cost.

The stock price is also dictated by the current stock market price when the employee is given the option of purchasing stocks. In general, stocks are held for a long time, allowing space for the value of stocks to increase and thus allows the stockholder to sell the inventories for profit at a later stage.

That is how stock options work: if a buyer buys a stock option, the buyer is given the right to sell or purchase a certain number of shares at a price negotiated on or before a set date, which is also known as the "strike price." He can decide what he wants in terms of stock, which leaves room for him to adapt his investment strategies to suit the current view of the stock market. Investors may use stock options on current stock holdings to gain more income and, in effect, defend them on stock depreciation. Options are exchanged on the market periodically, and the stock option premium rises at a much higher pace when the demand increases. The number of options on the market depends on the number of buyers and sellers interested in the selling and purchase of a certain stock.

CHAPTER FIVE

ADVANCED TRADING STRATEGIES

Are you looking for alternative trading options to help you with your investment projects? Do you want to handle your finances efficiently and make your money work for you soon? If yes, read on to see if you can find help with some useful to realistic trade strategies and other investment techniques.

A stock option is a derivative protection because the value of the option is "derived" from the common stock value. In fact, two options exist: calling options are options for the purchase of the underlying asset, while Put options are options for selling the underlying asset. In order to enable trading and price reporting, the listed option contracts are standardised. These stock options require the option holder to buy or sell 100 acts.

It is true that mixing option trading approaches can have impressive benefits and potential with limited risk for certain individual traders only if you have learned their concepts and principles and all the facts and knowledge that can be correlated with trade-in options. Let us look at some of the competitive advantages, the upside, and the downside of such a trading approach in greater detail.

Influence, and power. If you are using these strategies in trading options, it helps you to make such related investments without unnecessary funds in the broader portfolio.

Adaptability. In general, several areas can be extended and used in many options-trading techniques for almost every market environment or impartiality status. From its core trade strategy options to complex trade agreements, individual or single investors may choose for several different reasons and goals. Sure, you plan to take a hedge, to keep a single inventory option and a stock itself, to spread, take a position on two (or more) identical options, and to take a position on all calls and on the same stock on combination strategy. The decision actually depends on your hands, along with your investment portfolio and vehicle.

Complexity: The option trading strategies may be extraordinarily complex for the individual investor, and thus may not be worthy of your time, energy, and money. Because it can seem complex in nature, investors and prospects must undergo extensive research, learning, and training to do so effectively and efficiently. Novices and beginners need not worry about it; however, web tools can also be accurate, objective, and experienced, but you are looking more at people with precise configuration and straight-level thinking.

Every nation is making its contribution to revitalizing its economic status and making it progressive and productive. As the global crisis is apparently eradicated and as officials are doing everything possible to end poverty and financial instability, it is high time to learn how to maximize these opportunities simply by investing your money in good and reliable investment schemes. Learn how to trade effectively, invest now, and make your money work for you and your loved ones. Start today's passive income. Here's how the following is:

Know who you are and what you've got inside of it. Productive people are focused on this. You should set your financial targets and have a good idea of what you need and what you want today and tomorrow. It is crucial that you set your expectations-know your targets and know if you want these points by trading options. To be careful and practical is a good thing, but it's not wrong to dream big, because for you and your family only you deserve the best and the brightest. You should have the character and attitude to excel in all fields, in particular, in investment portfolios and other trade schemes.

Keep your assets separate and separate from your investments. They are not the same. You should bear in mind that your investments will be your assets, which may be used or reserved for emergencies as well as any emergency or out-of-list expenses; your investment and trading assets need to be a further collection of regularly reserved numbers. You have to draw a line between them. And this keeps your investment assets safe and untouched.

Save now. Time is a commodity, so you take already a wise decision when you begin trading or investing earlier. The sooner you invest, the better you make your money work for you, experts say. As the cliché goes, time is money, and take the chances now.

Get acquainted with the game, know and strengthen the game plan. Knowing the trading strategies and other available tools that can be used effectively and efficiently in investment and trading can seem like small but reliable beginnings. There is a greater likelihood to succeed and take advantage of your efforts. Learning from experts and experienced investors can be a great alternative. Learn and take it from your own experiences and insights.

As you find good and effective trade strategies for options, you are guided to this page and read this book now. These techniques are believed to be effective because when an investor or trader is equipped with appropriate expertise, experience, knowledge, and expertise for trade, investment, and other such projects, he or she can optimize its own ways of achieving financial success and stability. Get hooked up on this post and know the latest trends and tricks on how you can achieve financial stability at your own rate and convenience in no time.

In the first place, certain options trading strategies may appear complex, complicated, and advanced. However, once you join the game and know how to conduct the game plan, the means and other options trading strategies are maximized- one perfect way to learn how you and your finances will operate for your new projects. It is highly recommended, as a novice or as a beginner in trade options and investments, that you learn from the first-hand sources how to equip yourself with the right things to do, and set your mind and body to work towards another task which could lead you to more stable and safe finance in the future.

The only way to achieve these choices is to carry out a rigid study. Since we now live in the society in which technology and innovation have been useful and useful tools in providing us with reliable and valid resources-such inputs and references that we really can rely on and use, we can now just go online within a few clicks. There have been several ways to find creative and timely trading solutions – one which would meet the time requirements and requirements of your businesses.

In addition, there are growing numbers of people involved in investments, exports, exports, and the like, whether it be short-term or long-term plans and investment. With the determination, enthusiasm, skills, and expertise of the person, he or she can really add good benefits and edges to win this game. You must train yourself in all respects and areas before moving any of these companies beyond the effective and productive options trading strategies available and above all else. You must note that physically, socially, psychologically, intellectually, and spiritually, you have to brace yourself.

Reduce Your Losses By Learning The Advanced Binary Options Trading Strategies

Recently, binary options have revolutionized the trading landscape. Binary options have also become the preferred choice of the world's most experienced traders with their attractive features, such as enabling traders to start trading with limited capital and associated risk. There is no question that binary trading is the easiest to learn and perform, but it often makes a trader surprised when he has to lose because he lacks knowledge of profitable binary options. It is of serious concern that many traders enter the world of binary options trading without being advised by any viable strategies in binary options, and this is becoming the greatest obstacle to profitability in the face of market volatility. Learn the art of binary trading with the latest strategies for your success in this area.

Hedging - A Winning Binary Options Trading Strategy

One of the beneficial strategies to ensure that binary trading entails the least risk is safeguarded! The binary business primarily involves contracts limited to a few hours. Before a commodity expires, you can either sell or hold that commodity with you. You can now use either absolute or partial hedging to determine whether to sell the products. Full hedging allows you to sell the commodity or its entirety and to profit immediately if you feel that your investment is dangerous because of unfavorable market conditions. Partial hedging allows you to sell half of your shares and hold back the rest. Partial hedging is mostly applied when the trend line is moving to the general direction as per the trader's desire.

Straddle

One of the most used efficient binary techniques is a straddle. Straddle helps a trader to purchase the Put and Call options for the same implied properties. Now, at a high or low point, a trader crosses this particular asset. This factor maximizes the probability of success when the expiry takes place between the two points in the field. A differential trader would definitely use the Call option when the market is weak and use the Put option when the price rises. Therefore, a trader will make at least one profit from trade with the straddle while reducing the chances of loss..

Market Pull Strategy

This differential trading strategy allows a trader to be fully aware of the financial circumstances of various properties. A trader takes advantage of the economic calendar and studies the ties between the different properties. The market pull approach, therefore, just calls for a detailed understanding of the goods a trader uses for binary trading. The Web will provide traders with plenty of fantastic financial calendars that can be the perfect reference for a binary trader.

CHAPTER SIX

THE ADVANTAGES OF TRADING OPTIONS OVER STOCKS

Billions of dollars of shares are bought and sold on major exchanges around the world each day in the investment market. Every day, traders and investors will take part in the purest form of capitalism, jeopardizing their money by investing in benefits into some of the world's leading corporations. However, there is another way of speculating, trade options that can be much higher than simply trading a company's shares.

An option is a derivative for an underlying security that gives the right to purchase the underlying security at a fixed price but not necessarily the obligation. They come with different strike rates, maturities, and massive leverage as every option controls up to 100 shares of a particular company. These advantages make options even better than simply trading stocks.

One advantage is leverage. Leverage is the ability to leverage an enormous commodity with a limited amount of money. As in the case of real estate, where the prospective buyer is able to purchase a huge house, options allow the merchant to purchase up to 100 stock shares with a small bit of capital or in this case, it is called the "premium" option, which is the actual price of the option. Let us look at an example of how options are better than inventories by using leverage.

When you see the ABC stocks rally higher and sell $50 per share, then you purchase 100 stock shares for a total of $5,000. Some weeks back, ABC's stock has racked to $60, and you are selling all the shares that you've received $1,000 or 20 percent. Not too bad. Not too bad. But a friend of yours looks at the same set-up in ABC stock and wants to buy an option with a 50 $strike price that costs 2 USD for a total cost of 200 USD (2 x 100 USD = 200 USD). Your friend sells your $50 strike option for $1200, which is a 500 percent return! ABC stock rallies to $60.

That's the power of leverage when trading options.

Another advantage is that a trader can generate income through optional credit spreads. If you see that ABC is in a commercial range and is above support for about $50 a share, you can spread the credit by creating the so-called Bull Put Spread. You sell the current month's $50 insurance policy and pocket the premium you got, so you buy the $45 insurance option in the month to continue the stock plummeting suddenly. Sit back and let the options expire and collect the difference between the premium paid to sell the $50 set option and the cost to purchase the $45 set option.

ABC stock will go up or remain around $50 and make money from that position. This could even fall below $50 relative to the premium costs earned, and the place would even collapse! The only way the place could lose money would be if it dropped below this turnaround stage. Most traders of options specialize only in these options and sometimes produce steady returns of 10-90% per position!

A third advantage is that options also provide you with exposure to stocks with short-selling restrictions. When you cut off the stock, it's not just a bigger cash cost than buying shares, but you do have to pay interest on the stock you lent for short, plus you will pay the dividends the stock will pay back during your keep. You stop all that with options, and you can return much quicker and much cheaper because stocks usually fall twice as quickly as they go up.

Moreover, if a stock is expected to miss its earnings estimates, you can make a lot of money quickly by playing negative earning releases in the right market setting. The explanation is that stocks will always decrease in bad news by 50 percent or more. This translates into a big profit for a trader of intelligent options without a lot of money.

This also offers the key advantage is that the only premium you pay for the option itself is the most expensive one. When a stock falls in the news, and you're on the other side of the exchange, you risk just a tiny amount of money, and you could lose half of your profit overnight if you had bought the stock!

Google posted strong results early in 2006, but not as high as Wall Street predicted, and stock was pumped. Then a few weeks later, Google's Chief Financial Officer publicly spoke about a possible reversal in its potential growth, and the stock dropped. If an options trader were a long call option for Google at the time, the trader would only have lost a small portion of his trading capital to someone who purchased the stock himself (the Google stock had been up to $475 before these incidents, and lost nearly 150 points in a few weeks).

The Beauty Of Trading Options For Profit

There are two main reasons why people choose the trading route of options. It is to speculate or to cover up. This is a book that you can better understand the trading of options.

Speculation

The easiest approach is to think of speculation as a bet on a safety campaign. The major advantage of options is that if the demand rises, you are not limited to making a profit. There is a profit opportunity, even if the market "moves downwards" or falls.

There is a lot of money to be made (or lost) when it comes to trading, which is why it is regarded as one of the riskiest approaches to trade. The explanation is that you have to determine if the economy is going up or down, but when this happens, too.

But you do have to take part in commissions, and that is why it isn't easy to make money trading stocks because the odds are against you.

So why wonder people? Yeah, it's all about leverage; if you hold 100 shares in one contract, it doesn't need to invest serious cash on much of the price movement.

Then the other hand of the trading coin options is ... Hedging. Hedging.

Hedging

Consider this as an insurance policy. Like when insuring your house or family assets, options may be used to avoid market downturns for your investment.

Yeah, the skeptical people suggest that if you are so confident of a position on the market, why should you hedge? Nonetheless, it can be useful to hedge even for you on a small scale.

The technology sector, for example, is a competitive market. Say you want to invest in a technology business because you can see a big profit opportunity. Knowing the market as it is safeguarding is a means to limit your losses should your investment not work (say another company makes your company obsolete by breaking the technology).

Understanding The Advantages of Futures Options

The use of options has grown dramatically in the last decade. The value of options contracts traded on U.S. exchanges in 1999 was around EUR 507 million, according to data collected by the Options

Industry Council. By 2007, the number rose to over three billion, setting an all-time high.

However, future options are very risky strategies, which can be understood only by experienced traders, which may also be very useful for the individual investor.

Potential options will also add value to your portfolio and have some other benefits to be noticed. Several of them are listed below and help to explain why options have become so common in a fairly short period of time.

The first advantage of future options is that they will offer improved cost efficiency. Since they have huge leverage capacity, the investor can get a great option position that almost imitates a stock position but saves you unnecessary costs.

The second benefit is that if they are used correctly, they give less risk. Although there are circumstances in which options of purchase are potentially more risky than equity, they may also be used to reduce the risk. Potential options may be less risky since less financial investment is required than equities. They are also the most reliable hedge type that makes them safer than inventories.

The third advantage of future options is that they offer a higher return rate. It ensures that you will invest much less and make about the same profit from the underlying future as you would. It gives you a higher return rate.

The fourth and final advantage mentioned in this book concerns the strategic possibilities for the future. Options are a very flexible tool and provide many possibilities for restoring other positions. These are known as synthetic positions. Synthetic positions provide you with several approaches that can prove extremely useful for investors to accomplish the same investment objectives.

The above four points are the key advantages that potential alternatives offer and lead to their growing popularity. They pose less risks than straight futures if used properly and can potentially save you unnecessary costs while you make the same profit. This should be taken into account when selecting an investment type. You want to make the most of your money, and future options offer many ways to do this. Take the time to test this detail before you agree to buy it. Make sure you understand how the decision you make will help and what it will mean in monetary terms for you.

Consider the key benefits and weigh the risks of every opportunity against what you're willing to lose before you decide on a specific investment. Make sure to consider how to use potential choices correctly to make the most of them. You spend in your future so think cautiously and carefully. The closer you know, the safer and prosperous the future will be.

Advantages of Trading Options Over Traditional Stocks

Trading options are not as frustrating as others say. Trading options, as with anything, will require some learning and practice. Trading options are safer for many reasons than trading stocks. It is a fact that options for trading are considerably cheaper than the securities (where options are based).

An option contract allows you to manage an ABC business block of 100 shares. This contract in ABC Company costs you less than the purchase of 100 shares in the portfolio of ABC Company. I'll give you only one explanation (not just one), and a very significant one, in my view, why trading options are better than trading stocks. You leverage trading options! Through trade options, you have less capital investment and, at the same time, keep a greater share and buy shares directly in any given company. This gives you the ability to make bigger, lower risk, percentage gains.

Let's assume, for example, that you buy a $100 stock and sell it at $120, netting 20% more. You can purchase the $100 call option for the same inventory, and you will be paid $10. You could sell your option for $20 if the stock hits $120. It gives you a net of 100% and a chance of $10 rather than $100. The example I have just provided is a simplistic example, but the definition is not so complicated as most people assume. It should be a breeze if you are a successful day dealer or a seasoned stock trader. Even if you don't, options are worth a look, and you don't have to figure out. There are many places where you can set up stock and option virtual trading accounts. You may use these virtual accounts to learn the jargon and practice your business skills. Every virtual account you set up will have free tutorials that are really useful, and you can even get real money from some virtual account websites.

Investments are profit-oriented. A profitable venture should enrich investors with both experience and money so that unlimited opportunities are created. Trading of options for understanding comes into the same umbrella. An investor, particularly a beginner, must learn the easiest steps when it comes to the trading of options.

To begin with, understand the essence of the stocks. Options function in the same way as other securities like bonds and stocks but with recognized variations. For example, options are risky investments because money is involved. The same applies to other investments and securities. Although these common denominators exist, the trading of options requires more research.

Secondly, the distinction between putting and calling options must be understood. A call choice refers to the way a choice is obtained while the put option refers to the way it is offered. Options or options are complex investments, and the first step in knowing these securities is to know the fundamentals.

Third, trading of options refers not only to the knowledge of security or investment but also to the place of business where trading takes place. A bourse or stock exchange is essentially the location where stock options are negotiated by sellers and buyers. It is the area in which so-called investors learn to negotiate and deal with brokers.

Fourth, know the trading business language. A few of these definitions are terms such as premiums, maturity, expiry date, and uncertainty. Specific quantitative concepts, such as valuing options and out-of-the-money trades, also describe trading options. In the end, you will generally work your way to optimize any possible benefit by simply learning these simple words.

Fifthly, learn how to make money. Trading of options usually only becomes successful when outcomes are obtained. In this particular case, it's more about profits and benefit generation. Trading options occurs when options are sold or bought. In the meantime, gains are raised by receiving cash from supposed sales. The real aim is to make the most of a certain investment and constantly participate in the stock market, which is your path to financial success.

Trading options is like adding the icing on a served cake. It is the culmination of simple steps towards income or profit. You spend some money simply by buying options or stocks. From there, you can try and sell your stocks for possible income to another party. Others also note the potential for losses in options/stocks trading. Investment is, however, only earning money until decisions are fairly well interpreted and implemented.

CHAPTER SEVEN

STRATEGIES TO MAKE THE VERY BEST USE OF YOUR INVESTMENT CAPITAL.

Day trade isn't for the heart's faintness. Many times you'll be struck, but those with the skills to educate themselves on the best way to quickly buy and sell stocks will get a living from electronic trading a few hours a day. Apart from reading, studying, and exercising knowledge, a high-speed internet connection is needed so that no information is missed.

One thing all beginners need to realize is that capital should not be money to pay bills. Learning strategy and investing in a day-trading course and software that allows you to read the market or to handle a company account is a smart idea. Others go on day trading and learn from losses, but if you can continue with as much experience as you can, it means more money at the bank. Even if two people begin with exactly the same capital, they will invest it in very different ways. Just because a friend does trade in one way does not mean that the other person has to trade in the same way to make a profit.

It is necessary not to deter a trader from loss. Such losses are part of the trading lesson. Many businesses will offer a virtual account, which is a perfect way to practice what they have learned before you put real money into an account. Gain all from any mistake and change so that less mistakes are made. Profit is made if the investment prices are bought, but when the market crashes, day traders are still able to reap the benefits. This is known as 'shorting.' Even if a stock or bond loses, the trader wins.

Day trading isn't for people who want to dabble. A careful approach needs to be taken to make money. Once upon a time, there was no access to business without a broker. People now have access to the same information pro traders have always been able to access.

The Ultimate Top Tips for Creating a Successful Investing Strategy

What used to be a property of the wealthy now is available to almost anyone who wants to participate. Many have been burnt with opportunities and uncertainties of investing in financial markets. About 50% of investors own their own stock as "mom and pop." World governments are showing that people will take care of their own finances as public pensions are under pressure. Nobody needs to smoke their retirement.

Many people retire about half the time they live, work 40 years, and retire an average of 20 years. If you expect to live well at this time, it is important that you know about investment. You will also learn how the market works and inquire about its strategies if you go for a licensed investment advisor. Get to know the investment language to determine if a plan is right for you.

Perseverance is one of the greatest investment keys, don't bring something under the bed to save it, and don't hope to be rich overnight. Don't presume you can know anything immediately, but find the basic rules for productive investment:

1. Manage your own investments. You should not even let a stockbroker or financial consultant do it for you. You really know what you want and need, not your investment man like other stuff in your life.

2. Disseminate your investment, but not too much, to reduce the potential risk.

3. Don't just do what someone else does; try to be the absolute opposite. Find what they do and sometimes seek the opposite.

4. Don't be left in the cold when investors think about trade. Master the conversation.

5. Don't shy away from a potential uncertain market – now could be the best time to buy. Don't expect anything to change; that's when someone else will join.

6. Your heart will be high-quality shares and then go to the speculative areas.

7. You should also be mindful of the different implications for your potential tax payments while spending, but never let the tax minimization be the only or primary intention. Just seek to comply with a rational rule of thinking to that your tax returns as long as your investment is sound for certain factors.

8. Please read financial documents diligently and look for independent or unsponsored investment research sources to keep you up-to-date.

9. Investment conversations, even with those that make you feel lower, may be really interesting.

10. Don't be covetous or slip into the "just a little longer to see what's happening" pit. Be careful with yourself to cut losses as soon as they come from any poor investment and always cash in when you have made a fair profit - definitely so much so that, in those rare situations, your initial expenses can be covered with huge investments.

11. Patience is a virtue; today and tomorrow's penthouse, you won't be in the outhouse.

12. Don't believe in anything that you just don't understand. This is exactly what investments this sound 'too good to be true!' Prevent! Prevent!

13. Make sure you budget enough for yourself before saving. Today, the general way for the majority of people to spend their money is to take what they have left from paying the bills for that month and use it. Typically-they then notice that they have left nothing to pay for unnecessary transaction or cost in case of an emergency!

Strategies That Can Help You Beat The Stock Market

You should continue to learn new investment strategies as a stock investor. It may not work now what worked in the past. Tomorrow can not work what works now. As an investor, you will continue to learn new things. Buying and holding were one of the most popular investment strategies in stock in the past. Is it working anymore? Most analysts agree that the days of equity market purchases and holdings are over. Markets are now a lot more volatile. Yes, electronic trading has changed the very essence of the markets of today. Below are five stock market approaches that you can always use;

Stock Investing Strategy #1: Always Look For Those Companies That Others Are Ignoring

Don't go for overhyped stocks, always go for overlooked stocks that haven't even attracted investor imagination. Inventories overhyped are often overpriced. When you invest in them, a significant part of the possible price appreciation has already occurred. So why invest in them if you have already lost all of the potential capital gains. Invest in neglected stocks that have, for the moment, gone astray with the market, either because of any management issues that can be addressed in the near future or because of weak product launch. As long as the fundamentals behind that stock are strong, there is always a strong possibility of those stocks making a comeback with a bang. You need to do your research. Never invest in stocks without doing your research thoroughly.

Stock Investing Strategy #2: Use Charts To Time Your Entry And Exit

Time to get in and out of the market. Effective entry and exit are much more critical than a good selection of stocks. Suppose you had picked a very good stock, but it was wrong to enter and leave the market. What do you get, your stock's poor return? Know how to use charts to get in and out of business.

Stock Investing Strategy #3: Never use Market Orders only use Limit Orders

Don't just enter and leave Business Orders. The use of a market order means that the current market price is received. When you use the command on the market, your order will be filled at a price that is higher or lower than you thought when you ordered. This is because of the fast nature of the stock market, which always increases or decreases stock prices. Use Limit Orders and get the stock price you wanted.

Stock Investing Strategy #4: Keep an eye on the currency market

In today's global economy, financial markets are highly interconnected. Any instability in any other financial market will soon be overshadowed by the stock market. Take a look at other markets that can affect inventory prices in your inventory portfolio. Currency markets are important to check if foreign or international inventories are included in your portfolio.

Stock Investing Strategy #5: Always keep an open mind

Perhaps in the currency or commodity market, you can get a better return. It's still important to keep your mind open. Just go where you can get your investment's best return. Over the last decade, commodities have made higher returns relative to stocks. Similarly, you can make a stable 5-10% return on the currency market, which can easily be converted into an annual return of 60-120%. Compare this rate of return with the stock market rate that is probable.

Using Stop Losses to Boost Your Stock Investing Returns

This is the dream of each investor to buy and sell at the bottom of the market. We would all be very happy investors if this happened all the time.

Sadly, no one's happy all the time.

You can, however, continue to achieve the right investment strategy if you take losses with some of your stocks. You don't always have to buy at the bottom and sell at the top to generate sustainable returns if you obey the rules.

Let's check out the math. You will keep your portfolio ahead of the game if you reduce your investment losses by 7 to 10 percent and allow your winners to make a profit of 30, 50, or even 100 percent.

When a stock has been purchased, investors are inclined to assume that price declines (under purchase price) may be immediate, or even a small bounce, on a volatile market. This can also mean a steady downward trend in a troubled stock. Very rarely, speculation and hyperbola will build up a glamorous stock, but unfortunately, it has very little substance. During the tech boom, this situation was prevalent. Some creditors suffered tremendous losses while waiting for the turnaround. In many cases, this never happened.

Cutting losses through stops is a tough strategy. This is because investors tend (though they deny that) to get somewhat emotional about their shares. They bind themselves to the specific business and optimistically change things for the business. They don't sell these inventories unless they've wasted a bucket of cash already.

Reducing your losses is the best defensive strategy for any investor. When you successfully manage your stocks and keep a close eye on market trends, you can quickly see when stocks start to lose money. It may be a little bit now and then, but if a real downward trend is obvious, then the situation must be addressed. Using automatic stop losses will help compensate for the losing trades for psychological difficulties.

If the stock falls, say that you should be prepared to sell it immediately 7 to 10 percent below its purchase price. If an automatic stop loss has been created, the automatic loss will take place after the trigger point has been reached. You have to see a 33 percent rebound before you get even again when you stick with that stock until it comes down to 25 percent. When you skip this point and the stock drop 50%, you have to recover 100% before you even split.

When you buy a $1 shares stock, and it falls to 90 cents, get rid of it easily. Show consistency and commitment to your plan. Sometimes the stock you sell can rebuild afterward. Then you may regret selling.

Conversely, if you buy a stock, and it rises by 10%, you are prepared to sell the stock at a 5% decline, thereby holding 5% of its benefit. If it rises 25%, be able to sell the stock if it falls just 5%.

If your stock reaches a 25% increase, you may have a plan to sell anyway. There is no reason why this plan should not be respected. By changing your sales plans to lock in profits, you can avoid the situation that your stock that experienced a meteoric increase may then fall similarly catastrophically and wipe out any gains that you have made.

Using this technique sensitively, you can prevent major losses and also achieve good benefit.

A sale stop of 7 to 10 percent initially means that the investor can cope with any short-term market fluctuations. You can, however, also use stop losses to help you make a difference. This technique is called a stop loss trailing. You may claim to yourself that once you have made a large paper profit stock, you will sell by 5 percent. Every day after the end of the market, you adjust the loss to be 5% lower than the closing price for the day.

The main rule is that you should never that your loss. It lost all relevance as a trading discipline as soon as you dropped your stop loss. Of course, the stop loss must continue if the stock continues to grow-a a certain degree of adjustment is required, sometimes regular. At any point, though, if a significant profit is made on a stock (e.g., 50%), it is best to lock the profit with a loss of 5% when the stock peaks. This technique enables you to limit your losses while your profits are running.

Recall that while none of you lost money by taking income, unrealized paper gains were evaporated by many investors when the recent downturn muddled the stock prices. In uncertain times, stop losses can be a very useful tool for investors in maintaining capital but also to maintain profits in their most profitable companies.

Strategic Lifestyle Planning and Return on Investment

What is a business strategy for lifestyle? Just like a corporate strategy, a strategic lifestyle plan is a way to build your life in a systematic way that delineates what you want most.

As individuals, many people build their career plans and change their lives accordingly. Then they all get lost in everyday life and their relationships and lose sight of the big picture. That's why they always find it hard to find a balance in their lives.

By confirming your life in your job or company, you really spend a lot of time and energy on managing your life. You have almost created another job or business for yourself (full or part-time).

How you do continuously "finish" your life to suit your work, and I am not thinking about the economics involved with your professional lifestyle.

I suggest that you define your values, beliefs, and objectives in support of life and lifestyles-first and then plan your career or business around this strategy.

After this, you can think more clearly about how you spend your time, how you want to concentrate on the things that matter most to you and how things that really do not work for you are minimized or removed.

One way of looking at this is by using another conventional business metric or ROI. ROI is a measure of output used for the evaluation of the investment efficiency or for the analysis of the production of different investments. Every company's aim is to capitalize or optimize its total return on any investment.

As we learned, time in our lives is the new currency (LINK). Since time is money, we know that our time is our biggest investment. We can then apply a ROI standard to all that takes our time.

Would you ever reluctantly accept an invitation to attend a party where you really liked the hosts, but also, you wouldn't want the majority of the other guests? And wasn't that party as bad as you expected? A smarter plan would have been to meet the couple privately for dinner. What about when the buddy invited you and him to play a golf round and two others you wanted to meet? You suck on golf, you spent hours pulling your tail in the warm sun, and you had a horrible time because there was never a "right" moment to talk about it. Wouldn't it have been easier to expect a better chance?

It is not always as straightforward to find out how to invest your time, as I shared with you in real life lessons. Like with everything in existence, you just have to find your own way of doing things without "THE Answer," comprehensive math, or computer programs.

Here are some guidelines that help me decide how to invest my time (or how to analyze how I wasted my time, so I don't repeat the same mistakes again and again): I like to keep it straightforward.

Discover Win-Win Situations

I feel very lucky that every day I live a win-win scenario. Years ago, I found out that I like to deal with people and turn them into new things and ways of thinking. My own motto is to inspire men. I do this every day, not just in my company but also through my volunteer work. In both my professional and personal lives, I will follow my ideals and beliefs. It is the best win-win I can imagine.

A win-win in any scenario in which returns are high and can rise over time, and costs and losses are small and low compared to profit opportunities.

In Win-Win conditions, intangibles are often difficult to define and calculate, so look for. Many of them can also be a long-term bonus.

Win-Wins can be as simple as transforming your technical know-how, interest, or hobby into a cash-making additional profit, spending "downtime" – time you are in the doctor's office, switching or waiting, taking a podcast telephone or listening to a book you wanted to read. You might argue that the former doesn't qualify as "winning," but you are looking after business and doing something you choose to do. What could be better? What better?

Evade Lose-Lose Situations

This is clear. This is evident. I'm not going to a 9 a.m./10 p.m. movie because I get up at 5 p.m. and that bad decision will affect me professionally and personally throughout the next day.

There are free food and alcohol, I'm not going to a 'Networking After 5' event, because people generally focus on eating free food and drinking free booze, and once they get away from it. Too little "Networking" is really happening. Most of the food is usually fried, so I really don't need it, I don't drink, and it's a business event where almost no business is discussed - three strikes and I'm out. Again, my personal and business lives take negative hits - Lose-Lose.

Redeploy Your Assets

Time is just a commodity. We've just got so much of it. It's also dynamic – it's changing all the time, and so you are.

Asset redeployment is a method for relocating the assets of the company to improve productivity.

Personally, you must always be able to make the most of your talents, qualities, principles, opinions, ideas, and beliefs.

As you are always learning and growing, you need to be flexible so that your time is more productive and efficient. Always be able to reorganize, reassign, and redistribute your skills.

Determine Risk: Reward Ratios

This measure is used in enterprises to compare an investment's expected returns to the amount of risk accepted for these returns.

In fact, what does this mean? Most of us have been told that if we just work hard enough, our lives will finally turn out to be perfect, and everything will end up worth it. As a result, we often postpone things- we take a few risks-until the timing is accurate. We are accustomed to still delay things until "Thursday," since it seems like the sensible and least dangerous course of action.

Since it is always difficult to define the implications of action taken today, we are plagued by indecision. We make things more complicated than they really are.

Life is too late. Life is too short. The riskiest course of action is often to do or do the same. When we don't move and grow, we stagnate or fall back. We're wasting our precious energy.

Invest today your time. Try something different. Do something different. Life experience. Life experience. Do not look back at your life and hope that when you had the chance, you would have invested your time.

CHAPTER EIGHT

STEPS TO CHOOSE THE RIGHT STOCK OPTIONS

So everyone makes money selling options, and you want to switch from plain old boring stocks to trading options. This was good, but since you began trading options, you've been bombarded with the hundreds of options on every stock, and when choosing which option to trade, you can never seem to be making the right choice. This guide teaches you 5 basic steps to pick the right stock options for trading options.

Step 1: Decide on the outlook of the underlying stock.

There is no magic formula in options trading where the trend of the underlying instrument can simply be traded and profited without being concerned. The first step in selecting the right option to trade is what you expect the underlying stock to do first. In stock trading, there are typically only three perspectives; bullish, bearish, or neutral. However, there can be as many as six different opportunities to maximize income in the options trading industry; continuing bullish, mildly bullish, optimistic, volatile, enduring bearish, and mildly bearish. You need to decide on which of these six outlooks most closely conform to your expectation on the underlying stock as each of these outlooks require a different options strategy to best optimize its profit potential.

Step 2: Decide on the time frame of that outlook.

Now that you have decided what the underlying stock will do, the next question is WHEN you think the underlying stock will meet its expected expectations. This addresses the question of which month to swap your choices. The amount of expiration months available for a rising stock is one of the first things that disturb new option traders. Options are derivatives that expire once their lifetime has expired. It's not like stocks that can last as long as the company remains. This makes it so necessary to select the correct expiry month. Options become increasingly costly and less sensitive to movements in the underlying stock at longer expiration. That is why trading options are not as simple as trading options with the longest possible expiry. When you exchange options with an overly long expiry, you pay more for less and the return on investment. Conversely, if you trade options with an expiry period too short, you can end up with an expired position without any value even before your underlying stock is able to move accordingly. The more reliably you can predict whether the underlying stock complies as expected, the higher the return on investment in options trading. Situations such as income releases or some major announcements can be made to determine the exact time of the outlook. In addition to these objective incidents, it takes exceptionally strong analytical expertise and experience to determine whether an item will reach or stay within a price range.

Step 3: Decide on the magnitude of that outlook.

The size of a view refers to the degree to which you expect the underlying stock to shift in the anticipated direction. In the case of an expected neutral trend, the extent refers to both the expected length and volatility of this neutral trend. Therefore, the trading in options classifies bullish and bearish movements as either mild or persistent. Knowing the importance of the perspective helps you to determine the numerical value of the right to exchange. Money refers to how much money or money is a choice. The more expensive the money an option is, the less the leverage, but the higher the benefit is gained in minor price fluctuations of the underlying stock. The more the money an option is, the cheaper it is, the higher the leverage and the less prone it is to market changes on the underlying stock, which can be best used if the price movement is high.

Step 4: Decide on the optimal options strategy for your account level.

Now that you have an idea of what the underlying stock will do and how strong the transition might be, you will agree on the best option strategy to take advantage of that move. The best strategy for options can be either as easy as buying a call or setting an option or as complex as a double butterfly spreader. Your choice of options strategy will also be limited to the stage of your account trading, which determines your options strategy. This trading level account is calculated by your broker on a single basis based on the size of your fund and your trading experience.

Step 5: Decide on the exact option to trade, taking all of the above into consideration.

Having weighed all the above considerations, you will then be able to agree on the exact correct trade option. An example of how it works is given here:

When it is now January, and the stock price is $50. Suppose you think the stock's price will increase but only moderately to $55 next month. You agreed that this is a reasonably bullish outlook that can be balanced more effectively with a Bull Call Spread by writing out the monetary call options on the estimated price limit on money call options instead of just buy in the money call options. Taking all of these factors into consideration, you decided to execute a 50/55 bull call spread on that stock's March expiration options, giving a little bit more time for the stock to move to that expected price.

Understanding the Features of Options

While the risk of options trading is greater, many investors are attracted by the increasing opportunity for higher income. The appeal is comprehensible. You can easily make capital by investing in options if the stock increases in value. Naturally, because inventory prices can drop just as easily, there is an inherent and significant risk in investment options. If you are thinking of investing in options, you will have to be sure you are well educated, prepared for the risks, and ready to play.

If you purchase an option, you actually purchase the right to later purchase or sell a certain stock at a particular price. There are two options known as the "call" and the "put" for each option trading trade. Calls allow traders to lock in a stock price, knowing the price could be rising or declining. If the price increases, the customer receives the product for a lower price. You can sell your stock at a locked price if you keep a put. In this case, you would seek to lower the price, as you would receive a higher return on your investment.

Options trading is a complex business that requires you to be well informed before making any investments. Some brokers only allow professional investors to trade options, as the risks are higher. When you want to invest in options, you need to consider the possible consequences of both purchasing and selling carefully. It is typically better to purchase options than to sell options; however, in any case, there is no guarantee.

Preparing Your Finances for the Risk

Because the trading of options carries more risk than general stock trading, it is important that you have your finances in order before you start. It is best to have experience in other forms of trade, especially in the sale of stock. You should always be financially stable and mindful of how much you can afford to lose. Some investors take a portion of their profits from stock trading and start their trading options with this money. This is a smart way to ensure that you don't exchange too many properties unintentionally.

To begin trading, you should first study the market conditions and get to know the potential results you could face. The complexity of options for many investors is an exciting aspect of the trade. You will have to be willing to play and understand that you can end up with substantial gains or losses.

If you think the trading of options is the correct decision, try to test the water by putting a small investment in a low-priced option. This gives you a sense of the market and process that can serve you and move to higher-priced choices. As you move on, seek the resources of your online broker to develop a long-term strategy. With the right strategy, a business eye, and the ability to take a gamble, you can make a considerable profit by buying and selling options.

Why Most People Fail at Options Trading

Have you or your friends ever participated in an options seminar, learned how "easy" it is to generate high income from trading options, but when you did it really, you failed to consistently make money?

In fact, my observation of the last decade in this industry has shown that the chances of success for start-up options dealers are extremely slim. Only a very small percentage of people make money consistently from options trading in options, as in all other life. This is valid even for beginners who have taken the same choices. Yes, some people will actually take advantage of the trading of options even with participants of the same options, although most won't. What went wrong? What went wrong?

I examined why the trading of options failed and reduced it to two main reasons;

1. There is no proven, and systematic approach novices can follow and trade with finances and economics.

2. Absence of a robust business mindset.

Let's admit, most traders of starting options are not professionals. Indeed, most don't even have financial or cultural backgrounds and don't understand why things happen in the stock market or the economy. For beginners, learning to pick inventories and evaluate trade can be a catastrophe because they lack full information. There's a lot of beginners failing here. Yes, it is a tragedy even for experts, to discretionarily take stocks based on a set of hypotheses that do not fit together in the first place or pure intestines. To ensure that beginners are reliable in trading options, a stable, detailed and unbiased trading system and structures that cover all aspects should be implemented so as to obey rules and make very limited subjective decisions or evaluations. Such a framework should include an objective method of identifying potential trade opportunities, an objective method to identify the correct trade options for optimizing trade risk/rewards, an objective method of assessing whether an entry should be made, and objective profit-taking and stop-loss policies. No non-professional options trading beginners may expect to produce a consistent return without a purposeful, validated program and structure.

Today, the "made for beginners" trading system is clearly the basis for success in the trading of options. The trading mindset of the traders themselves is what really defines long-term success. Where is the point of a trading program if the trader can not obey the rules? In fact, many options are offered to beginners who, in the past, have suffered such losses that they are usually governed by fear and emotion in so far as they are unable to follow the rules at all. If the approach that you follow allows you to join when a stock breaks out, a voice in your heads prevents them from buying and suggests that the stock will actually dropdown. Then they watch the stock go up until it is too late to enter.

For successful options traders, a certain psychological profile is required, which includes the ability to listen to the rules of their chosen trading system and technique, regardless of how they feel. We need to be able to get rid of the money we sell, much like a doctor's indifference of their patients' cries. A good business mentality is not by its very nature. It's something you should practice. Traders with great choices look after their life in general and focus on stress management and relaxation in their everyday routine. Conversely, there are also traders who have lost so much on the stock market that they can typically no longer control their emotions and trade controlled. Yeah, there are, sadly, people who should stay away from trading options.

CHAPTER NINE

HOW TO SEE PATTERNS IN THE MARKET

Recently, almost no trading seminar is without any technical analysis or introduction. In fact, almost all the trading options of blogs on the internet are the key basis for technical analysis. What is it? What? Why is the trading of options so closely linked to technical analysis?

To understand the important link between technical analysis and options trading, we first need to understand what technical analysis is doing.

There are two main analytical methods: basic analysis and technical analysis.

The basic analysis is to read fundamental business or economy data to forecast and invest in potential company or market results. Such key data include profit and loss statements, income growth, and income guidance. The underlying issue with research is that large corporations do not always stock a lot. Stocks of big companies also undergo downturn periods, often for prolonged periods. As a result, an investor will primarily decide on stocks to buy for the long term (5 to 10 years out) if nothing unexpected occurs in the years that follow. Indeed, fundamental analysis is a favorable tool for investors buying dividends and dividend growth stocks.

Technical analysis (TA) is the examination of stock market data. Yes, while Fundamental Analysis is a company analysis, TA only studies its stock. These market data include price over various times and transactions in volume. Options traders see from price and volume how the stock's price does not matter what the company data does. This helps traders and investors avoid these extended downturn periods, although the fundamental data of a company appear to be great. Indeed, while a major analysis tells an investor who is a good company, TA tells an investor when it's time to purchase or sell stocks. Indeed, the strength of the technical analysis is its ability to guide investors' purchasing and selling choices through price patterns and price trends over short periods.

Why, then, is technical research such a preference for trading options?

Let us note that basic analysis is conducive to long-term investment and technological analytics are ideal for use even in short periods of time. Options traders will still retain stocks, but after a set period, options expire. Sure, options usually last just a year, and options traders often use option trading strategies that require months or weeks to require extremely short perspectives. This is why technical analysis is so closely linked to the trading of options. Options traders simply have no luxury to maintain a position as stock traders for years. In addition, options traders do not receive dividends like stock investors. The only way to make money in the trading of options is to make an anticipated forecast during the expiry of the options. This makes the company's fundamental strength fairly unimportant. In addition, options traders will benefit if stocks also fall. This also makes it relatively unimportant to identify good companies through fundamental analyses. Indeed, reading market movements and demand patterns, which may indicate the direction in which a stock moves the next week or month, has greater value than reading a declaration of profit and loss that does not tell you where the stock might be for the short term.

Steps For Profitable Call Option Trading

Many traders want more sophisticated trading options, but often the simple trade of calling options is the best trade for the market condition. Follow the steps below to increase your likelihood of taking advantage of calling options.

1. Determine that the price of the instrument underlying it rises. The call choice is a directional approach. This means that you have to choose the course of the market, and the market will step up to profit. There are several ways to predict the upward progress of the market. Some people respond to good market news and use basic information such as higher income per share, higher dividend rates, higher income etc. Others use diagram trends that display upward market movement, including dual foundation, reverse head and shoulder, upward triangle, and upside price breakout. Many systems use other methods such as Elliot waves and methods that use market fluctuations combined with other indicators.

2. Determine the price movement target. The system you use to signal a rise in prices should also define a target movement level.

3. Take the time to switch to your target price for the underlying product. How long do you expect the prices of the underlying instruments to rise towards the target price? This is important for determining the expiry of your calling options.

4. Look at the chain of options. Bring out the quotes and other related data options chain. Real-time options chains are now conveniently accessible via the internet. You can also call your broker to get this information.

5. Enter the exchange and expiry date. If you are trading online, decide the exchange you wish to position your order. Determine the appropriate expiry date based on the time the price is expected to move. Without a trading system that trades options close to

expiration, you normally want to buy call options that are slightly longer than the expected time. This reduces the effect of the decay of time. This is very important because time drop can lead to a loss of value for your call options.

6. Compare the Delta, Gamma, Vega, and Theta at the same expiration of several strike prices. After you have reduced your chain of options to a specific exchange and expiry date, look at the Greeks. You would prefer high delta, high gamma, low vega, and low theta. When the underlying price moves up, high delta and high Gamma can give you a higher and faster profit. Low Vega is very relevant when you buy options. Low Vega means cheaper options, and you make a profit when Vega increases even if the underlying price does not move. Low Vega is linked to low volatility and quiet market conditions. And low Theta means that the call alternative causes smaller time losses. If you're a long-term trader, you can pick call options out of the pocket. These are smaller delta options, but less expensive. If you're a shorter-term investor, you'd rather call money or money because they can produce higher profits and quicker because of the higher Delta and Gamma.

7. Assess your risk against rewards based on your target price. You can also use a risk profile to help you conduct the assessment. Using this formula to measure your breakeven point: breakeven = call strike + call premium

8. Look at the value and volume that are available. Trading in an active market is easier, because you can quickly buy and sell. Another reason is that you don't lose much in the spread of the bid/work.

9. Select the best calling option with the highest profit probability.

10. Determine exit and stop-loss points. Before putting your company, ensure that you have your profit taking points and avoid losing points in place. Do this so that after you enter your business, your emotions will not take over your decision-making.

11. Place your business. Call your broker or key online in your company.

12. Track the price movements of the instrument and the market reaction of the option

13. Close your position. When you make a profit, close your position either by selling or exercising the call option, the call options you purchased and sell your shares. If there is some time left before expiry, it is usually best to sell the call options because the value of time is still there. Close your position by selling the call options when you make a loss.

How to Read a Candlestick Chart in Option Trading

Candlestick is one of the most reliable indicators that traders and investors always use when they want to make decisions. That is because the candlestick is the only predictor tracking the movement of a specific stock when the market opens. It will create a candle when the price is closed in some time. Other indicators just wait until the candle is created and follow the trend. Here are several Candlestick Candles terminologies that we typically see in the table.

Bullish English: The candle of bullish (white) is replaced with a bearish (red) light. It occurs when the market is opened; when the candle opens the same or lower closing candle, the candle closes higher than the previous candle. Every time we see this pattern on the upward trend, the entry is confirmed.

Bearish Engulfing is the opposite of Bullish Engulfing's pattern.

Doji is indecisive, which means that the candle is opened and closed. We have to wait every time we see such a trend because there is no proof.

Bullish Harami is a bullish candle (white) shorter than the bearish candle (red). All you need to do is wait for the next candle if the next candle indicates that it's higher than the previous candle on the upstream. It is an entry confirmation for the upstream location.

Bearish Harami is the opposite of Bullish Harami's pattern.

In reality, I don't talk about more trends in the candlestick map. It is because the patterns I list above are the most accurate method for trading options.

Market Trend Analysis for Options Trading

Almost all of the traders of options have heard the old commercial adage saying, "The trend is your friend." In reality, trading options against the current market trend certainly put the chance of winning in your favor. Too many start-ups have lost their entire accounts by purchasing call options in a bear trend market and purchasing options in a bull trend market.

So, what exactly is a market trend?

Trends in the market are like ocean tides. You know it's a rising tide when you see the sea rise higher and higher and when you see more and more of the ocean, it's a falling tide. Similarly, you know that this is a bullish trend when you see major indices such as the Dow Jones Industrial Average or the S&P 500 going up, and when you see the main indices falling down and down, you know that it is a bearish trend.

Yes, market trends are general directions in which inventories appear to move. In a bull's market, the prices of most stocks are rising higher and higher, and the price of most stocks is decreasing and decreasing.

One thing about trends, however, is that trends are a "Common Movement Leader." It does not mean that the market is up in a bull cycle just every day and does not mean that in a bear cycle, the market just goes down.

If you watch the sea tides rise, the water does not tend to rush to the ocean, but falls in "Waves." One wave is stronger than the last. The same is true of stock market patterns. You can see days interspersed with days in a bull trend. However, notifications should occur more frequently and render new highs after each mild retreat.

This fact often surprises new traders who interpret bull trends as "the turning bearish" on the first day of the day. This is also the case in the proverbial bull-trap and bear trap, both newcomers and seasoned options traders, who are short counter-trend developments misinterpreted as trend shifts. Traders who fall into either pit are generally shocked if the general pattern persists, and they are stuck in a losing position that can never be reversed.

Recognizing how patterns actually work is just the first step towards business trends understanding. Have you ever come to the conclusion that the market just disagrees in one direction? How can two people in the same market draw different conclusions about the trend in the market?

The complexity of recognizing market trends is that the market can really be in all three directions at any time on the same day!

For day traders, the market may be a trend, but on the same day, it could be a bull trend for a swing trader and a neutral trend for a long-term investor. How can that be?

Actually, not only one "Market" condition but numerous market conditions depending on the timeframe on which one is trading! It is not known that the consumer trend for different trading and investment goals is different and that this leads to pointless claims about the market's trend on TV.

When you have software for charts, you might be shocked to see that often, depending on which time frame you are looking at a different chart pattern on a single index or stock; 1 min chart, daily chart, weekly chart or monthly chart, each one seems to tell you something else.

A diagram that is extremely bizarre in the 1-minute graph could look extremely healthy and bumpy in a daily diagram. The analysis of trends, therefore, requires an understanding of the precise time frame in which you trade. The exact time frame you are trading is an extremely important prerequisite for trading options where the contracts for options and the positions you purchased are time-sensitive! Yeah, options do not last forever, so all options approaches have an optimal timeline for an optimized return.

When you trade daytime options and either write or buy options to close it off for profit by the end of the trading day, for example, the market trend you should be concerned with is the intraday trend most commonly identified with minutes. Whether the market is in a long-term cycle of bulls or bear, it no longer affects your trade. The universe can be screaming, but if your minute charts are daring to the day, the way from which you make your money is bearish.

If you are selling a covered call, you might want to buy call options on an inventory that is fairly side-by-side on daily charts for market trading across a range of daily charts, if you want to avoid the inventories.

Ultimate profit secrets that will guarantee your success

Most traders enjoy monetary options, limitless income, and restricted risk-theory sounds fantastic, but 90 percent actually expire without interest!

Don't play with options! Gamble with options! Take this basic scenario into account.

You bet on a horse race and have a favorite 3:1 and a 15:1 outsider. What is the safest bet? Well, bet on the outside, and you're more likely to win, but betting on the favorite gives you a better chance to win.

How often do you see a broken betting shop?

We do not know the chances of success very often, and the betting chances reflect that. It's obvious! It's obvious! Bet on the best. Bet on the least.

Options and odds for currency

For currency options, traders still make the long-shot outside bet.

You buy money options with a short time to expire, and that means that the chance of winning depends on Lady's luck.

If you want to place the odds in your favor, you need trade options for fewer potential gains, but higher chances of success and this requires two considerations:

1. Buy at or close to the money

Don't take the long shot; buy money options or in the trendy markets.

This way, you have time to correct and move in the right direction and remember that the trend is more likely to continue than to reverse.

The odds are more in your favor if you do this, and what the trading of currency options means.

Brokers and gurus want to make you like and appeal to your greed, don't listen, don't stick with money currency choices only, and the trading trends – where it's best for you to succeed2. Make time on your side

FACT: The shorter the time the monetary options expire, the greater the time decay effect. Many traders believe that these options are cheaper (cost-related) but not likely to succeed!

Make sure you spend plenty of time on your side and keep it.

Buying money currency options in or on a large amount of time value will cost you profit potential. But the potential not to be cash in your bank is just that-the potential, bearing in mind the situation of horse betting earlier. Do you know someone who bets and constantly wins on outsider? I don't. I don't.

Keep potential profit realistic. Alright, so you have less potential for profit, but you have more chances for success.

Let's now look at the right approach.

3. How to trade with odds of 90% success

Note that 90% of the currency options purchased expire without interest.

On the other hand, the individual who sold the option has a profit probability of 90%.

The real way to make money is through the sale of options. What options are you selling?

You have known it! Money options with a short expiry time.

In fact, selling options looks like a poor bet – there is an infinite possibility of a little gain, but keep in mind the chances are incredibly stacked for you.

Consistent huge gains

You need to be well-capitalized and swings against you in the short term to sell currency options. However, if you sell money options with time decline to kill them and spread your risk, you can save time and money.

This is not the science of rockets! You get nothing for good on financial markets, restricted risk, and the infinite bonuses of currency options come at a cost. It's common sense.

Understand this, and you are well on the road to making big money profits.

If you are a small trader, you are patient, and you are likely to achieve lower potential gains. If you are a large trader, you can sell and use the majority of the mug traders who want to give you their money.

Monetary options will make your money go along with the above-mentioned and get the odds, that's what you can do in financial trading so you can make big profits over time.

CHAPTER TEN

RISK MANAGEMENT

Risk management includes defining, assessing, and prioritizing the threats or uncertainties and ensuring that the effect of threats is minimized, monitored, and managed or strengthened by the use of co-ordinate and economical tools.

For every organization, risk management is important. It provides foresight for investment returns and projects every potential setback for a company by starting a new (or even routine) effort.

Five steps must be taken first to evaluate the risk and the best solution before determining the most effective risk management strategy for your situation.

Identify the risk

Risks include events that cause problems or advantages. Risk identification starts from the sources of domestic problems and benefits or from competitors. Risks should be internal or external such that the program can be used to recognize the different possible risks.

Analyze the risk

Once you have identified risks, the possible effects each has on consumer behavior, your business, and other current efforts can be analyzed thoroughly.

Evaluate the risk

You can now allocate a rating quality to the likelihood of results of each risk. This helps to explain how a project or new product is seriously threatened by a risk. You can also determine the extent to which each risk can destroy or support a new tactic. The magnitude is a combination of the probability and effect of the risk.

Treat the risk

You will begin to handle the worst risks first, so you are conscious of all potential risks and their severity. First, you want to see if you can decrease the probability of a negative outcome and then how you can raise the chance. Prevention and contingency should be prepared at this stage in the risk assessment so that no surprises are found as you move forward with action plans.

Check the risk

You know the threats, the probability, what happens if they happen, and how to avoid disasters. What next? What next? Control the risks by monitoring the variables involved and proposing potential chain reaction hazards. As your system detects changes, treat the problem calmly to prevent large-scale onslaught effects, and to trigger a high risk.

It takes us to the next big risk management wave: risk control. There are several ways of treating risks, and they all depend on what kind of risks are addressed and how serious the effects or opportunities are. Let's look at techniques. Let's look.

Best strategies for treating the risk:

Evasion

Best case scenario, you can absolutely eliminate risk impacts. However, you also forfeit all risky activities and all the associated potential returns and opportunities. What kind of danger operation you want to experiment with is up to you.

Lowering

Risk reduction introduces small changes to reduce both the weight of risk and the reward after the event. The reduction requires some process and plan manipulation, but in the event of a high-risk event, it saves your company from a serious loss.

Share

Risk-sharing or transfer redistributes over multiple parties the burden of loss or gain. These can include representatives of a corporation, an outsourced business, or an insurance policy.

Conservation

Danger retention implies the full expectation of loss or gain. This choice is better suited to small risks where losses can easily be sustained and compensated.

When we speak of risk, we refer to the possibility that an adverse event may arise and its consequences for us.

It must be made clear that since this concept is quite broad, we are only going to refer to financial risks, to explain how we can control those financial consequences that are negative for a business.

Types of financial risks.

- Market risk. Associated with the variations suffered by the financial markets, and in which we can distinguish:
- Currency risk: they will be the consequence of the volatility of the currency market.

- Interest rate risk: they will be the consequence of the volatility of interest rates.
- Market risk: to refer more specifically to the volatility of the markets for financial instruments such as stocks, debt, derivatives, etc.
- Credit risk. One that refers to the possibility that one of the parties to a financial contract does not fulfill its contractual obligations.
- Liquidity or financing risk. It covers the fact that one of the parties to the financial contract cannot obtain the liquidity it needs to assume its obligations despite having assets (which it cannot sell) and the will to do so.
- Operational risk. The possibility of financial losses, whether due to a failure or insufficiency of processes, people, internal systems, technology, etc.

There are 3 ways to take a risk:

- Transfer the risk: We transfer the risk to another party, by selling that asset or by contacting an insurance policy.
- Evading risk: Simply do not expose yourself to the risk that has been identified.
- Retain the risk: We directly assume the risk, and we will have to make the decision of how we are going to cover the possible losses.

Neither of these strategies is more advantageous than the other; everything will depend on the type of activity we are carrying out and the type of risk they are aimed at.

How to decrease your financial risk? Control and management.

It is normal if you are an entrepreneur who tries to minimize the risk that your company may run, so as not to run into long-term financial problems.

This is one of the issues that entrepreneurs most often worry about when talking about the company's livelihood. And we fully understand that because the entire company could fall apart just by making a mistake.

It is impossible to completely eliminate the existence of risks, but it is possible to reduce it. For this reason, and going straight to the point, we have made a list, short but very useful, that will help you, if not to reduce, at least to be able to control and manage the risks that your company runs.

Evaluate the profitability of each investment. This is something you should never forget. You have to always keep in mind that the more information you have about the operations, the lower the risk.

Anticipate the future. We know that this is impossible, but referring to the previous point, we may get very close to what can happen later if we have great information to help us compare situations, decision-making, and strategies.

Diversify. Something fundamental that can never be lacking in any risk control strategy is diversification. We can do this by proposing investments of various types, for example, highly dangerous investments that compensate for others of very low risk. This will make you have a broader investment portfolio and that you can obtain better results in a safer way.

Evaluate the results obtained. You should not forget this; it is very important that every time you obtain the results of the operation, you study them carefully to analyze what is happening. This can also help us predict the future!

It has a professional team . Managing your accounts deserves specialized knowledge of new financial trends.

You can always protect some of your assets by taking out insurance.

The hedging. Along the same lines as diversification, we can also combine some assets from the same portfolio, with the aim that the variations of some counterbalance those of the rest.

Establish coverage. We refer to those operations that consist of currencies other than the euro, where a variation in the price can surely have a high financial cost.

Tips to prepare for a possible financial crisis

1- Free yourself from debts

In times of economic crisis, financial institutions often turn off the tap to grant credit as protection. It is one of his techniques for different clients who have debt capacity from those who do not.

Reaching a critical moment with a high level of debt is not beneficial at all, so it is advisable to pay them off as soon as possible and not take on more debt.

2- Choose the right time to buy a home

Acquiring a home is one of the most important decisions we make throughout our lives, specifically for the mortgage loan that will surely be associated with the purchase and will accompany us for at least two decades.

Waiting for the next stage of recession to happen to invest in real estate does not have to be a good decision because perhaps in the next crisis, prices will remain stable, and there will be no room for "bargains." It may also happen that prices drop, but mortgage interest rates soar.

When is the ideal time to buy a home then? The one in which we are able to face mortgage payments without our home economy suffering a great effort.

3- Promote savings

As small as it may be, starting to create the habit of saving every month is essential to build a small mattress from which to survive in the event of an unexpected economic setback.

It is recommended to save at least 10% of each of the income we receive each month.

4- Plan for your retirement

In other countries like the US, creating an investment plan for when you reach retirement age is something that is integrated into your culture, and the profitability of pension plans grows steadily most of the time.

In our country, we are not so far-sighted, and the great variety of pension plans makes many of them unreliable, leading to ruin. The best advice? Be well advised on the product to be invested in.

The trends are divided, on the one hand, there are those who predict a new and close economic crisis, and on the other those who take iron out of the matter. The best advice in the face of uncertainty is to be forewarned.

5- Clean up your treasury

For companies, having a healthy treasury with which to deal with unforeseen phenomena is increasingly important. Among the circles of financial experts, there has been a tendency to affirm that «Cash is king» or what is the same, having an excess of cash and liquidity is the best umbrella for when a storm is coming.

How to earn money on the stock market: the keys

Let's put ourselves in the situation. From a theoretical point of view, money is made on the stock market if one of these two things happens :

You buy shares of a company at a price (for example, 20 euros) and, after a time (days, weeks, months or years), you sell them at a higher price (for example, 25 euros). In other words, you buy cheap and sell expensive. This is what all investors are trying to achieve.

Through the distribution of dividends from the company in which you have invested, that is, when it decides to pay its shareholders.

In practical terms, investors can use various "strategies" to make their investment profitable. These are not tricks in the strict sense of the word, but rather ways of operating on a day-to-day basis to earn money. Let's see three quite recognized:

How to earn money on the stock market: Buy & Hold

It translates as "buy and hold" and what it comes to mean is that you should buy when nobody wants to do it and keep what you have bought no matter what happens and for as long as possible until you can sell at a much higher price.

This method requires maximum discipline for two reasons: first, you should not check how your investment is going on a daily basis, with doing it once or twice a year is more than enough; and second, you have to put your mind in the long, long, long term and not sell before 20 or 25 years. The stock market in the long term is always profitable; you just have to maintain it.

How to make money on the stock market: Surf the ups and downs

This method consists of looking for winning trends in the medium term, that is, between one and three years, even up to five. It is an investment job that requires patience and prior knowledge. Technical and fundamental analyzes are essential to finding these trends.

Just like a surfer looking for a good wave, when investing with this method, you have to look for a good trend, even if it means weeks of waiting. Upon finding it, you invest in it and wait for the wave to grow enough. When the change in trend is detected, a conservative position is adopted and sold.

How to Earn Money on the Stock Market: Trade as a Trader

It is the most complicated option of all and the one that requires the most discipline—the traders operating in hours, days, and weeks. The most successful are intraday traders, that is, those who buy at the beginning of the day and sell when the market closes. Logically, volatility is maximum in such short spaces, and it is very difficult to find well-defined trends.

By operating as a trader, you can earn money steadily but also lose it in the blink of an eye. The stop loss is essential to prevent the latter from happening.

In any case, the great advice that we give you is that you get good advice before investing in the stock market. Not everyone is capable of doing it on their own. In fact, a large part of the investors who go to it without the professional help of an expert end up losing money. Don't let the same thing happen to you.

Questions you have to ask your financial advisor to know if you can trust him

Most people who invest in the stock market do so by putting themselves in the hands of a financial advisor. This expert guides them and indicates which are the best investment products based on the risk they want to take and the return they want to obtain. The problem is that it is difficult to find a good financial advisor since most of them are "married" to a specific financial institution. To find out whether or not you can trust your advisor, we suggest that you ask the following five questions.

What are the total expenses that I will assume?

It is the most important question of all. The investment is not free and involves a series of expenses that must be known in advance. In addition to being very clear about what the price of the advisory service will be - and if this is per consultation, per hour or the delivery of results - you must also know the total costs of the products in which you invest, as well as the costs of the internal transactions of the funds, the currency exchange or the forks that are applied in the purchase and sale.

Keep in mind that in financial advice, the total free does not exist, so if a financial advisor offers you 0% of expenses, he is lying to you. Only big fortunes will get commissions below 0.5%. For the normal investor, a margin of between 1.5% and 2.5% in expenses is normal. Fewer expenses would be very good, and more expenses are not justifiable.

How will you diversify my investment?

If the financial advisor proposes to invest all the money in a single company, in a single country, or in a single sector, he is possibly speculating. You should run away. A good advisor will propose to create a globally diversified portfolio that includes many companies from different sectors and from different countries, as well as fixed income, both corporate and public.

Could you show me an example of a plan you made?

It is important to know the work and specialization of the financial advisor in whom we are going to place our trust and what better way to do it than by studying some of their current jobs. A good advisor should show us, in addition to extensive information in the form of text, also tables and graphs with the returns of different funds and products depending on the risk that we assume we want to assume.

What will be the tax impact of my investment?

It is as important to know the profitability of the investment as the taxation linked to it. The advisor should update us on this aspect and explain with hair and signs the invoice that we must pay to the Treasury for the benefits that we obtain by investing our money. You can not imagine the surprises that many people who invest in pension plans get when the time comes to recover the money.

What information will I have access to?

Before, investment was a bit taboo and difficult to understand. Thanks to the internet, the opposite is true today. It is no longer necessary to visit our advisor from time to time to update us on our investment, but rather to have the right online tools to check how our money grows from home.

However, that does not mean that the advisor should be there to resolve any doubts that arise. Therefore, it is important to be clear how often we will receive updates on our investment. There are advisers who send information monthly, others quarterly, and some annually. Many advisers also send general investment information to their clients so that they learn, for example, about how financial markets work.

CHAPTER ELEVEN

THE MOST COMMON INVESTOR MISTAKES

Moreover, according to several studies, about 90% of individual investors are losers in the long run, and success is constant for a minimal part of them. I will now look at some of the main reasons for your potential failure as an investor.

Trying to get rich quick?

Your investment horizon must be an eternity. The stock market and other stock markets are a good place to increase your savings and secure your antiques, not to get rich quick. If your goal is the last one, then you better try your luck in a casino; there, even your chances will probably be higher.

Eligible investments are those with at least a two-year investment horizon. Any investment that looks like it could double your money in a month or two is probably very risky or a "pyramid scheme."

This type of investment usually leads to large capital losses if you make a mistake, so avoid them.

Calculations show that by making 15 deals a month with a yield of 5% each, investors would turn $ 1,000 into 276 trillion dollars for three years. In reality, however, this is impossible.

There is no way to realize continuously profitable deals for such a long period. It is possible to turn a thousand dollars into hundreds of thousands or even millions, but the key to achieving this lies in perseverance, patience, and time.

You use too much-borrowed capital (leverage)

Usually, investors use borrowed capital, driven mainly by their desire to get rich quick. Generally speaking, leverage is money borrowed from your broker, which allows you to trade with funds many times the amount of your equity.

Many times, more means one hundred, two hundred, and sometimes even higher numbers such as 500 and 1000 times. Leverage helps investors multiply their profits many times over.

There is only one small problem. It is that leverage increases not only profits but also losses of investors. When using large leverage, a single mistake leads to a complete loss of capital.

I must point out that currency brokers can now be found offering leverage of 3,000 times the amount of your funds, and there is even such a bidding, "infinite leverage."

In other words, if you have an account of BGN 1,000, thanks to the leverage of BGN 3,000, you will be able to open a position in the amount of BGN 3,000,000. Sounds great, right?

However, how long you will be able to withstand such a large position is another matter entirely.

It is likely that the logical question will arise in the minds of novice investors, why are brokers so willing to lend such amounts?

There are several possible answers. First of all, by opening larger positions, you will pay higher fees and commissions to them. Secondly, they really want to make you rich, because again you will pay higher fees and commissions to them.

There is another third reason that few people talk about, namely that many brokers simply do not "cover" the positions of their clients, which benefits from the fact that 90% of them will lose the money that will go into their pocket. These types of brokers are called market makers. Think carefully, do you want to use the services of one ?!

And do you think that you can always know?

If yes, then why leverage? A small percentage of profits each time, for years, will make you rich, even if you start with small amounts. I.e., you don't have to use leverage!

If, after all, you think that even ingenious investors like Warren Buffett make mistakes and the answer to the question, "Can you always win?" It is "NO," then again; you should not use borrowed capital. Because with a high value of such, you will increase your loss from a single error to an insurmountable value.

For example, if you use standard leverage of 100 times, a move in the currency pair you trade 1% in your direction will bring you 100% profit or double your funds. Sounds easy, right? This is ultimately only one percent.

But what happens when the currency pair falls by 1%? You lose all your initial capital.

Moreover, to maintain your position, the broker will most likely ask you for additional collateral (margin call) before reaching this one percent, and if you do not deposit additional funds to maintain your position, it will be closed a lot earlier than reaching this 1%.

Do you know how much the currency pair has to move to lose everything? If you use, for example, a margin of 1000 times - 0.1%. This is within market fluctuation or statistical error. In other words, the market can "erase" all your capital, even then move in your direction.

In general, it can be concluded that the use of unreasonable leverage is the basis for 90% of investors to lose.

As Warren Buffett says, many people fail because of alcohol and leverage. Leverage is the use of borrowed capital. You really don't need leverage in this world. If you're smart enough, you'll make money without borrowing, the Omaha Oracle advises.

You set unrealistic goals

Is 5-10% a good return? In 2017, this was not the case. However, given the low-interest record rates worldwide and the record-high levels of many of the world's leading stock indices, this can be said to be a good annual return. Don't be greedy because greed is a bad counselor and will often make you take reckless risks.

You start trading with big capital

Especially if the markets are something new for you, you should not approach them too confidently and arrogantly. While researching and studying them, invest a small amount. This will protect you from insurmountable losses. You will certainly have such, do not be fooled.

Even if you start with a few very successful deals, this is not a guarantee of long-term success. Good asset management and iron discipline are two of the key factors for good results over a long period of time. However, until you get them, do not risk much, especially your entire savings.

Don't follow your risk profile

Before you start trading, you need to determine your risk profile or risk tolerance. In other words, how much you can afford to lose without it being critical.

Investors often face a problem. Even if they correctly define their risk profile, they subsequently assume a higher level of risk than what they are tolerant of (most often due to "drunken judgment"). This is why they are often tempted by the temptation to follow another investor with a different tolerance for risk.

The fact that your acquaintance has earned a yield of 50% per year does not mean that you can expect similar results. When comparing with other investors, first compare whether your risk profiles are the same. Is your tolerance for loss the same, and what are your time horizons?

Bad investors see every loss as a failure. And who loves failures?

However, small and controlled losses should be seen as small victories, namely that the small loss is not allowed to become insurmountable.

Good investors know this - losses are part of the game, and small losses don't matter.

Professional investors or those who trade the stock markets properly to have long-term success always have an exit strategy. They do not try to prove in every way and at all costs (of all their capital) that they are right, because they know that they can be wrong.

And one of the best strategies for getting out of a losing position is with the so-called "stop losses." These are orders to limit losses at certain levels.

For example, if you buy a stock for $ 10, and your exit strategy is, in case it brings you a 10% loss, then you can put a "stop-loss" at a level of $ 9 in advance. So, if this price is reached, which you are most likely convinced will not happen, you will know that you made a mistake, and triggering the order will get you out of the losing position.

Your ego is too big

The big investor ego, in other words - the confidence that you can't go wrong in the market, is often the basis for using borrowed capital in your investments. When you think something is 100% safe, it makes perfect sense for you to use leverage to increase your profits.

The investor ego has misled more than one investor and is a factor that largely predetermines us to make the same mistakes. Ask David Einhorn, for example.

You are trading with funds that you will need soon.

It may seem like a good idea to increase your child's college savings on the stock market, which you will need in two or three years, but this may not be the case! Especially if from this amount, you can not afford to lose a lev.

As Buffett says, your investment horizon must be "eternity," or at least ten years. Otherwise, you risk entering the so-called "spiral of eternal losses."

This is when you sell at a small loss (with normal market fluctuation or correction) because you panic, then buy when the market goes up and sell again when it returns a little and so on indefinitely or rather until you lose your money completely.

And this happens because the invested funds are firstly extremely valuable to you, and secondly, you know that you will need them in a short period of time.

Unfortunately, this is another common mistake that costs us dearly and makes us regret it later.

You bond emotionally

Don't "fall in love with your choice." In fact, this is a very common phenomenon. Like our life and our tendency to be attached to someone with whom we spend most of our time, so in the markets, we become attached to the company we have chosen, the more we read and are interested in it.

Differentiate yourself from your emotions and seek the opinion of other experts to see if your judgment is blurred.

You do not "collect" profits

Investors often succumb to "greed" when the shares of their companies move in the desired direction.

They are inclined to abandon their set goals for leaving the position in the hope that the actions will continue in the same direction. Thus, the most appropriate moment is often missed, and the trauma of "unrealized gains" makes them make new and new mistakes.

You do not judge the best time to sell.

How to hit the best time to get out of position? Read, read, and read again. When you do this, read a little more. What you read is like "insurance"; the more you practice it, the more protected you are from mistakes.

You lack discipline and patience

Lack of discipline and patience dooms almost every investor to a total loss. You may have hit the right moment to enter an asset. However, all the benefits of this will be lost if you sell it earlier before the full potential of the position is fully developed.

Another way in which a lack of patience affects investors is to rush into the market before the direction has changed in their desired direction.

Here is an example of this. The US S&P 500 was close to a record high as of October last year. All market participants had the feeling that we would see new peaks. However, the lack of patience made many of them shorten the index despite their expectations. This brought them serious losses when the index continued to rise.

You are over-trading

Not having patience will make you susceptible to another serious mistake - "overtrading." This is a situation where investors experience inconvenience and discomfort when they are out of the market. Thus, in addition to paying large commissions to their brokers, they often get involved in losing trades just because of the "action."

CONCLUSION

Options are rights to purchase and sale of an asset (stocks, stock indices, commodities, raw, etc.), called an underlying asset. There are two types of options: Call options; they are purchase options. Put options; they are sale options. This means that options can be made in both bull and bear markets, and even in the side markets. The options are very flexible, and just as they allow you to take very risky positions, they also serve to reduce and control risk. There are many strategies that use only options, or stocks (or any other underlying) and options in combination, the risk of which is lower than that of buying ordinary shares. The risk that is taken is always determined by the investor; nobody takes more risks than those that they want to take. Anyone who knows the workings of the options, which is at the reach of anyone, know exactly the risks involved in each operation with the choices you make.

www.ingramcontent.com/pod-product-compliance
Lightning Source LLC
Chambersburg PA
CBHW070241220526
45465CB00004B/1481